It Happened to Me

Series Editor: Arlene Hirschfelder

Books in the It Happened to Me series are designed for inquisitive teens digging for answers about certain illnesses, social issues, or lifestyle interests. Whether you are deep into your teen years or just entering them, these books are gold mines of up-to-date information, riveting teen views, and great visuals to help you figure out stuff. Besides special boxes highlighting singular facts, each book is enhanced with the latest reading lists, websites, and an index. Perfect for browsing, there are loads of expert information by acclaimed writers to help parents, guardians, and librarians understand teen illness, tough situations, and lifestyle choices.

Living with Cancer

The Ultimate Teen Guide

DENISE THORNTON

It Happened to Me, No. 30

The Scarecrow Press, Inc.
Lanham • Toronto • Plymouth, UK
2011

Published by Scarecrow Press, Inc.
A wholly owned subsidiary of The Rowman & Littlefield Publishing Group, Inc.
4501 Forbes Boulevard, Suite 200, Lanham, Maryland 20706
http://www.scarecrowpress.com

Estover Road, Plymouth PL6 7PY, United Kingdom

Photo of Amber and Megan appearing on alternating chapter opening pages is courtesy of Amber Luchterhand. Photo of Libby appearing on alternating chapter opening pages is courtesy of Elizabeth Falck.

British Library Cataloguing in Publication Information Available

Library of Congress Cataloging-in-Publication Data
Thornton, Denise, 1949–
  Living with cancer : the ultimate teen guide / Denise Thornton.
    p. cm. — (It happened to me ; no. 30)
  Includes bibliographical references and index.
  ISBN 978-0-8108-7277-6 (cloth : alk. paper) — ISBN 978-0-8108-7278-3 (ebook)
  1. Cancer in adolescence—Juvenile literature. I. Title.
  RC281.C4T56 2011
  616.99'4—dc22   2010044140

∞™ The paper used in this publication meets the minimum requirements of American National Standard for Information Sciences—Permanence of Paper for Printed Library Materials, ANSI/NISO Z39.48-1992.

Printed in the United States of America

This book is dedicated to my brother, William Eric Thornton, whose possibilities were cut short by leukemia.

Contents

Acknowledgments

This book is built upon the generous contributions of many cancer treatment professionals and young cancer survivors who have generously shared their experience with me to make this book possible.

I am forever indebted to the young adults who revisited some of their darkest moments in order to light the path for other teens who must follow their footsteps. Their courage and insights have fueled this project, especially Kenzie Derr, Libby Falck, Jon Michael Gabrielson, Addie Greenwood, Peter Greenwood, Brittany Hill, Amber Luchterhand, Megan Luchterhand, Amanda Nicholls, Prisca Patrick, Seth Paulson, Chase Prochnow, Chelsea Prochnow, Justin Thomas, and Juliette Walker.

Thank you also to Toni Morrissey, senior media specialist of UW Hospital and Clinics, who facilitated my meetings with Sandra Bakk, parent/family advocate; Joyce Kilgore-Carlin, pediatric oncology social worker; Peggy Possin, coordinator of the Long-Term Survival Clinic; Andrea Urban, pediatric oncology social worker; Dr. Carol Diamond, Dr. Diane Puccetti, and Dr. Joel Wish, all associate professors in the University of Wisconsin–Madison School of Medicine and Public Health; and Dr. Paul Sondel, professor in the University of Wisconsin–Madison School of Medicine and Public Health.

I also want to thank my husband, Doug Hansmann, and my daughters, Della and K.J., who are all skilled writers in their own fields, for their emotional and technical support. Thanks ultimately to my wonderful editor, Arlene Hirschfelder, for unfailing guidance and assistance.

Introduction

The image of a young child with cancer yanks on everyone's heart strings. But cancer is especially challenging for teens. They must battle their disease while negotiating the tricky terrain of adolescence. At a time when they are reaching for independence, they can suddenly become as needy and helpless as a toddler.

Each year seventy-two thousand teens and young adults are diagnosed with cancer in the United States.[1] This book will explore the kinds of challenges cancer places on both those teens who have cancer and also teens who have friends or family members with cancer.

For those of you coping with cancer, these chapters will weave together the kinds of facts you need to make good decisions, along with glimpses into the journeys other teens have made as they cope with cancer. Many young cancer survivors have opened their hearts to build this book. Let me introduce a few of them here.

Peter Greenwood, a college student who lost a leg to cancer, says, "Lots of kids think they are invincible. Cancer will change your mind about that. You have a lot to live for, and you don't want to give any of it up. During treatment, I tried to make sure I enjoyed all the time I had, and I still feel that whatever you are doing in life, that's a pretty decent philosophy. You need to have your bigger goals, but you can't forget about this moment right now and make it count."[2]

Seth Paulson, a twenty-one-year-old lymphoma survivor, agrees. He says, "I sometimes think people take life for granted.

People always get mad about little things, but you should cherish those little things because you don't know if something like this is going to happen. You might get cancer or get in an accident. You don't know if your life will be taken away the next day, so you have to live every day to its fullest. I don't care who you are—you have to be aware of that."[3]

Jon Michael Gabrielson, a college student and cancer survivor who battled leukemia as a child, says, "Cancer shaped who I am. Listening to music was what I did in the hospital. I'm really into music today. I want to be a writer, and that developed from all the movies and books I went through during treatment."[4]

Amber Luchterhand, who has battled cancer twice during her teens, says, "What have I done in the past year? Some people earned great scholarships and have already completed their freshman year of college. Some are engaged or married. Some went straight into the workforce—straight into the real world. What about me? I don't feel like a normal teen. I missed out on a lot that I wish I could have experienced."[5]

Justin Thomas, cancer survivor and Alabama Young Hero says, "Rule number one: Never give up! I had everything going for me with sports. I had just been in my first school play, and two months later it all came to a shrieking halt. I had to change my life plan really quick. I started writing poetry and songs. I auditioned for another play. I'm a theater major now."

"With my cancer I grew up really fast," Justin continues. "That year molded me into the person I am today. It made me realize that my life was almost over before it began, and it made me take things for serious. People ask my why am I so determined and working so hard. I intend to take advantage of everything I do from this point out."[6]

These young people and many others will fill the pages ahead with their successes and their failures. I hope their stories will help you make the best of what can only be a very challenging time. Every person I talked to has a different story, but one thing they all agree on is that cancer makes you grow up fast, and that it can make you become more than you ever thought you could be.

NOTES

1. National Cancer Institute, "Adolescents and Young Adults with Cancer," www.cancer.gov/cancertopics/aya/types (accessed January 2, 2010).

2. Peter Greenwood, interview with author, August 20, 2008.

3. Seth Paulson, interview with author, August 26, 2008.

4. Jon Michael Gabrielson, interview with author, December 7, 2009.

5. Amber Luchterhand, interview with author, October 7, 2008.

6. Justin Thomas, interview with author, December 15, 2009.

1 **You Have Cancer**

No one ever forgets hearing the words "You have cancer."

All the teens in this book have heard those words. Finding out that the upset stomach, fever, or mystery pain is not something with a quick fix but cancer is probably the scariest moment of anyone's life. The important thing is, you are not alone, and there are plenty of places to get help for what is ahead.

This chapter focuses on what it means to learn that you or someone you love has cancer, how doctors can tell you have cancer, and how it feels to deal with what can seem like the worst moment of your life.

Doctors often start trying to figure out what is going on in your body by asking about your personal and family medical history. They will probably need to do a physical exam and take blood samples for testing.

If they see something that looks like a tumor, they may do a biopsy. That means that if they don't like the looks of a certain area, they remove some tissue so that it can be examined.

Your doctor may take tissue for a biopsy in one of three ways:

1. **A fine-needle aspiration is what most people have. Your doctor removes a sample of tissue with a thin needle. An ultrasound device can help your doctor see where to place the needle.**
2. **The doctor may use a thin, lighted tube (an endoscope) to look at areas inside your body. The doctor can also remove cells or tissue through that tube.**
3. **A surgical biopsy may be needed if a larger sample is required. The doctor may remove the entire tumor or just a part of it.**

I remember walking in the door. My mom had gotten the call while I was gone. I saw her face, and I knew that second. I went and lay down and thought, "What is my life like now?"

—Peter Greenwood[1]

WHAT IS CANCER?

Cancer occurs when cells start growing out of control and do not die when they should.

Cancer is not just one disease. The name covers more than one hundred types of cancer. Cancers are usually named for the organ or type of cell in which they start. For example, liver cancer starts in the liver. Carcinoma is cancer that begins in the skin or in tissues that line or cover internal organs. Leukemia is cancer that starts in the blood-forming tissue such as the bone marrow and causes large numbers of abnormal blood cells to be made and enter the blood. Lymphoma and myeloma are cancers that begin in the cells of the immune system.

Cancers begin in cells. Your body is made of many types of cells. They grow and divide exactly how and when you need them. When cells get old or damaged, they die, and new ones grow to replace them. Cancer is the name for what happens when the normal process goes haywire. The genetic material of a cell may be damaged or changed and start producing mutations that throw normal cell growth off kilter. Suddenly, cells are not dying when they should, and new cells that are not needed are being produced. There may be so many extra cells that they form a mass of tissue called a tumor.

Not all tumors are cancerous.

Benign tumors usually do not come back when they are removed. They don't spread to other parts of the body. Benign tumors don't usually threaten your life.

Malignant tumors are cancer. The cells in these tumors are dividing like crazy, and they can invade and destroy the tissue around them. Cancer cells can also break away from a malignant tumor, travel through your body in your bloodstream or lymphatic system, and attack other parts of your body.[2]

After tissue is removed, a pathologist (a pathologist is a doctor who identifies diseases by studying cells and tissues under a microscope) will examine it to see if there are any abnormal cells.[3]

People whose cancers are found early and treated quickly are more likely to survive their cancers than people whose cancers are not found until symptoms appear.[4] That makes it tough for kids and teens because people rarely suspect cancer

YOU ARE AN AYA. WHAT'S THAT?

Cancer has a special relationship with an adolescent or young adult, also known as an AYA, which is the term medical people use when they are talking about you.[5]

An AYA has been defined by the Report of the Adolescent and Young Adult Oncology Progress Review Group, who are your best friends. They understand your needs. Because they are also scientists, however, they had to define who you are. They have determined that AYAs are people aged fifteen through thirty-nine at the time cancer is diagnosed. Since the types of tumors that AYAs get overlaps with the cancers that affect younger children and older adults, there is really more than just a number involved in who is an AYA. Here are some of the things that make you an AYA.

- AYAs have a sense of invincibility that can make a cancer diagnosis hit really hard.
- Usually, AYAs haven't had a lot of experience with disease in their lives yet.
- AYAs are moving into independence as they get a driver's license, live on their own, graduate from school, get a job, and gain voting privileges and legal independence.
- AYAs are thinking about starting relationships, careers, and families—all things that cancer can derail.
- AYAs have to grow up quickly when cancer is diagnosed.[6]

when a student cramming for a test gets a headache, or a hard-charging young athlete suddenly has extra-sore muscles.

Peter

I graduated from high school a semester early and started taking college classes. I was a pretty competitive person, always playing basketball and soccer with friends. My left knee started giving out on me. I had never had problems like that before, so when it kept happening, I figured I should go to the doctor.

They told me it was probably tendinitis and would respond to physical therapy, but they would take an x-ray to be safe, which was really lucky they did. Immediately they could see something on the x-ray that wasn't supposed to be there. I had an MRI and then a biopsy. It was a needle biopsy and was really pretty painless. I remember the oncologist saying that day, "We'll see what this is. Hopefully it's something benign, and I'll never see you again." Instead, she's been with me every step of the way.

We knew the next day. I remember walking in the door. My mom had gotten the call while I was gone. I saw her face, and I knew that second. I went and lay down and thought "What is my life like now?" It was completely overwhelming. But I was immediately ready to fight. It's part of who I am way beyond the cancer. In sports, I am way more competitive than I need to be about getting a ball through a hoop, and this was my life, not a basketball game, so I was more determined than I have ever been about anything.[7]

*   *   *

Doctors use a lot of different tools to hunt for cancer. Sometimes x-rays can show the location, size, and shape of a bone tumor like Peter's. If it looks abnormal, they will go on to a special imaging test. They might use a bone scan, in which a tiny amount of radioactive material is injected into a blood vessel and travels through the bloodstream to the bones, where it is detected by a scanner.[9]

Juliette

I was 16. Before it happened I was really in a phase with swimming and school and everything. There wasn't really much wrong with me. I was healthy and swimming fast and running and doing lots of stuff.

I wasn't getting regular periods, and my hormones were always acting up. I had really bad acne. I went to an endocrinologist. After blood tests and an ultrasound test, they found a tumor in my ovary.

At first, they didn't think it was cancerous at all, so I didn't think it was that big of a deal. I was going to have laparoscopic surgery [laparoscopic surgery means the operation is performed through a very small incision], but the tumor was more solid, so I had to have major abdominal surgery. They found it was cancer, but they told me it would be fine after they got it out. Then a week after my surgery, they found that it was a really small, rare kind of tumor, so I had to have chemo. Each step of the way it progressed and got worse. I wasn't ready for it at all. I didn't expect anything like that.[10]

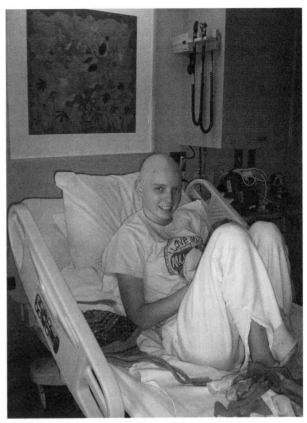

Juliette, diagnosed with ovarian cancer at age sixteen. *Courtesy of Juliette Walker.*

✳ ✳ ✳

Your doctor may use an ultrasound test. The ultrasound device uses sound waves that can't be heard by human ears. The sound waves produce a pattern of echoes as they bounce off internal organs. The echoes create a picture, called a sonogram, of your organs. Tumors may produce echoes that are different from the echoes made by healthy tissues.[11]

Amber

It was the summer before my freshman year of high school, and I was feeling really tired—just not really myself. My mom took me to the emergency room one night because I had a really

WHAT IS A PAP TEST ALL ABOUT?

A Pap test (sometimes called a Pap smear) is a way to look at cells collected from a woman's cervix (or lower, narrow end of the uterus). The doctor needs to see these cells to look for cancer or abnormal cells that might lead to cancer. This test can also find noncancerous conditions such as an infection.

A Pap test can let a woman know if she has abnormalities that might turn into cancer so that they can be treated before cancer develops. Like many types of cancer, cancer of the cervix is more likely to be treated successfully if it is detected early.

A Pap test is done in a doctor's office, clinic, or hospital. While a woman lies on an exam table, the clinician inserts a speculum (an instrument used to widen an opening of the body to make it easier to look inside) into her vagina to widen it. A sample of cells is taken from the cervix with a scraper or brush. The sample is sent to a laboratory for examination.

According to the National Cancer Institute, women should have a Pap test at least once every three years, starting about three years after they begin to have sexual intercourse but no later than age twenty-one.

About 55 million Pap tests are performed each year in the United States. Only about 6 percent are abnormal and require medical follow-up.

Pap smears can also detect human papillomavirus, or HPV. Some HPVs cause the common warts that grow on hands and feet. Over thirty types of HPV can be passed from one person to another through sexual contact. About fifteen HPVs can lead to cancer.

HPV infection is more common among young women in their late teens and twenties. Because HPVs are spread mainly through sexual contact, risk increases with the number of sexual partners. Most HPV infections appear to go away on their own; however, persistent infection with cancer-associated HPVs increases the risk of cancer.[12]

high fever, and they found that my blood counts were off. They admitted me to the hospital, did a bone marrow test, and they found that I had acute leukemia (cancer of the blood cells).

When we were waiting for the results of test, I was so certain that I didn't have cancer. When the doctor came in to tell me, I knew right away from the look on his face that the news wasn't good. He took my hand and told me I had cancer. Everything was a blur. I think I did cry. More than anything I was worried about how I was going to tell my friends, and what it would mean for my future.

I remember my relapse more clearly. My mom and I went in because I was having headaches. They did a spinal tap, but I already knew I had relapsed. The doctor came in and said it had

LANCE ARMSTRONG LEAVES CANCER EATING HIS DUST

Lance Armstrong started racing as a swimmer, and at age twelve, he finished fourth in the Texas state 1,500-meter freestyle. Then he switched to triathlon competition, adding biking and running to his routine. By age sixteen Lance was a professional triathlete. It seemed like nothing could stop him. His biking made him famous. Lance started taking home wins that no American had ever achieved before, but then in 1996 his performance began to suffer.

The reason became clear when he was diagnosed, at age twenty-five, with stage 3 testicular cancer and that cancer had spread to his lungs, abdomen, and brain. Though Lance immediately had surgery and chemotherapy, his doctor gave him less than a 40 percent survival chance.

Lance Armstrong did survive and surged back into competition with a thrilling comeback. He went on to win the 1999–2005 Tours de France. Maybe more important was what he did off the race track. During his treatment he created the Lance Armstrong Foundation and used his celebrity to become an advocate for people living with cancer. He says his new race is finding a cure for a disease that kills six hundred thousand people a year.[13]

The Lance Armstrong Foundation has a website called LIVESTRONG. It has a valuable page called "Find More Resources" that covers topics from emotional and physical concerns to coping with school and evaluating treatment options. You will find the website at the end of this chapter in the resources section. This website can help you learn more and find help.

The Lance Armstrong Foundation can help you with emotional and relationship issues. Check the resources section at the end of the chapter. You can use this site to find online, telephone, and face-to-face counseling. The site also offers a booklet that can answer your day-to-day questions called the *LIVESTRONG Guidebook*.

Lance's site even has a page that can help you find clinical trials that you might be able to take part in through his LIVESTRONG Cancer Clinical Trial Matching Service. There is a link in the resources section at the end of the chapter. And there are also links that can help you deal with the legal and insurance issues that cancer can force you to consider.

You can connect with the Lance Armstrong Foundation through e-newsletters, Facebook, and Twitter.

gone to my central nervous system. I cried one tear and that was it. I just decided I was going to fight it.[14]

* * *

Your doctor may remove some of the fluid that fills the spaces in and around the brain and spinal cord. To do this the doctor uses a long, thin needle to remove the fluid from the lower spine. The procedure takes about thirty minutes and is performed with a local anesthesia. You will have to lie flat for several hours afterward to keep from getting a headache.

Seth

It all began two years ago during my first year of college. I was eighteen years old, and I was having trouble breathing and chest pain. It was scary. This had never happened before.

It was November 2006 during our first big blizzard of the year. I remember I was with a friend, Joe. We were heading down the road because my friend wanted to buy a PlayStation, and I told him, "I feel really weird. For some reason, I'm having difficulty breathing."

I called my mom, and told her that Joe was taking me to the medical center in our town. My mom met me there. I was really worried at the time. I thought I had pulled a muscle lifting weights a few nights before. The doctors did tests. I got some blood work done and x-rays. Eventually they came back and told me there was, like, a dark spot on the x-rays near my heart.

I was still feeling crappy, and they put me in a room where I could lay down while they did more tests. They ended up calling an ambulance to take me to a bigger hospital. In the ambulance, they put a blanket on me and took me on a stretcher. The snow was still falling.

When they first put me in the ambulance, they didn't use the sirens, but when we got deeper into the city, that's when they turned the sirens on, and that was pretty heavy.

When I got to the hospital, the doctors did more tests. I was scared. I didn't know what was going to happen. I didn't think I had cancer.

When I was a kid I always heard the word cancer, but I never knew what it was. When they would say "someone has cancer," I knew that was not good, but I didn't really know what it was. I thought if someone got cancer, that they would die. I thought it was automatically fatal. I didn't realize it could be cured.

I remember when the doctors came up to me and told me what was going on. I remember my mom was there and my dad and sister came too. My dad was in tears because he didn't know what was going on. He came up to me and said, "Are you doing all right?" And I said, "Dad, I'm doing fine. I'm just a little tired." They started an IV. They ended up doing a cardiogram where you can actually see your heart, but there was nothing wrong with my heart.

I felt better and went back to school, but the next day my mom called me in the morning and told me I had cancer. My first reaction was to start bawling. I thought my life was over. I didn't know what cancer was. I just knew that it could kill you. It was scary.

VIRUSES, BACTERIA, AND SEXUALLY TRANSMITTED DISEASES AS CANCER RISKS

Some viruses and bacteria have been linked to several types of cancer.

A sexually transmitted virus called human papillomavirus (HPV) is the primary cause of cervical and anal cancer. Though both men and women can get HPV, if you are a woman who began sexual intercourse at age sixteen or younger or have had many sexual partners, you have an increased risk of infection. HPV infections are becoming increasingly common. HPV is the primary cause of cervical cancer, but most HPV infections do not result in cancer. You may not even know that you have an HPV infection because most of the time HPV does not cause any symptoms. The only way to know for sure is to see a doctor or nurse.

Hepatitis B (HBV) and hepatitis C are viral infections, and they are major causes of liver cancer. The rising number of liver cancers in the United States is thought to be due to HBV. You put yourself at risk for HBV through injection drug use and unprotected sex with multiple partners.

Epstein-Barr virus (EBV) is the virus that causes mononucleosis, and it is also linked to some types of lymphoma. Almost all adults are infected with this virus without it hurting them. The risk of cancer for people infected with EBV is pretty low, except for those whose immune systems are weakened, such as people infected with HIV (human immunodeficiency virus), the virus that causes AIDS.[15]

She was crying, and I was crying. I remember my mom told me, "We are going to get through this. It's nothing to be afraid of. We'll take it one step at a time, as long as we have hope." My whole family was 100 percent. The people around you are the ones who help you get through the day.[16]

* * *

Your doctors might also use a CAT scan (computerized axial tomography), which creates a detailed series of pictures of an area inside your body by linking a computer to an x-ray machine. Another way your doctors can get a look inside is an MRI (magnetic resonance imaging) machine, which uses a powerful magnet linked to a computer to create detailed pictures without using x-rays.[17]

Justin

I was diagnosed with B-cell lymphoma the summer after my seventeenth birthday. I had been having pains all year, but I was an athlete. I played football and wrestled. I got into theater too. I also played the lead that year in *A Lesson before Dying*.

> ☑ **COMMON TEEN CANCERS**
>
> **The most common types of cancer seen in adolescents and young adults are lymphoma, leukemia, germ cell tumors (including testicular cancer), melanoma, tumors of the central nervous system, sarcoma, and breast, cervical, liver, thyroid, and colorectal cancers.[18]**

I felt the pain as early as '06, but I didn't say anything till the next June. It's kind of common for athletes to have pain and not say anything, but my doctor said, the next time I have pain to let him know immediately. And I will.

A month after the play finished, I was at work, and the pain was getting worse and worse. When I started crying, I figured something was wrong, and I'd better get to the doctor. I never cry about anything.

I asked my boss if I could go, and I went to the hospital. About one in the morning they got to me. They told me there [was] a large mass on my spleen, and they want[ed] to admit me and figure out what it [was]. The next day they did a biopsy and told me it was cancer cells.

Honestly I didn't care. The one thing on my mind was sports. I was so passionate about sports, and I had just had the greatest season ever. My football team went to the play-offs [for] the first time in years, and I was being looked at by schools—being recruited. I was third in the state for wrestling and pre-ranked number one for my senior year. All I could think of was "I can't play sports anymore."

I haven't played since my last match when I won the state medal on February '07.[19]

Amanda

I was diagnosed when I was fifteen in my first year of high school. I have a really rare cancer, cutaneous T-cell lymphoma. It was discovered because of my track picture from eighth grade. There was this red spot showing, and my mom asked me about it.

I had always had skin conditions my entire life. I showed her, and she took me to the doctor. He did a biopsy, and I came back, and he was like, "You have cancer."

I felt pretty bad. My grandfather died of leukemia. I thought I was going to die. I thought my life had ended, but I have learned to live with it.

People need to know that just because I have been diagnosed with cancer, doesn't mean I'm going to die.[20]

* * *

NOTES

1. Peter Greenwood, interview with author, August 11, 2008.

2. National Cancer Institute, "What Is Cancer?" updated May 11, 2009, www.cancer.gov/cancertopics/what-is-cancer (accessed December 30, 2009).

3. National Cancer Institute, "Introduction," *What You Need to Know about Cancer*," posted October 4, 2006, www.cancer.gov/cancertopics/wyntk/overview/page7 (accessed December 30, 2009).

4. National Cancer Institute, "Early Detection," *Cancer Trends Progress Report—2009/2010 Update*, page last reviewed April 15, 2010, progressreport.cancer.gov/doc.asp?pid=1&did=2007&mid=vcol&chid=72 (accessed December 5, 2010).

5. Roni Caryn Rabin, "In Cancer Fight, Teenagers Don't Fit In," *New York Times*, Health section, March 15, 2010, www.nytimes .com/2010/03/16/health/16canc.html?hp (accessed March 17, 2010).

6. U.S. Department of Health and Human Services, National Institutes of Health, National Cancer Institute, and LIVESTRONG Young Adult Alliance, *Closing the Gap: Research and Care Imperatives for Adolescents and Young Adults with Cancer*, Report of the Adolescent and Young Adult Oncology Progress Review Group, NIH Publication No. 06-6067, August 2006, planning.cancer.gov/ library/AYAO_PRG_Report_2006_FINAL.pdf (accessed December 5, 2010).

7. Peter Greenwood, interview with author, August 11, 2008.

8. Charlene Laino, "Cancer Signs in Teens Often Overlooked," MedicineNet.com, October 9, 2009, www.medicinenet.com/script/ main/art.asp?articlekey=106403 (accessed March 17, 2010).

9. National Cancer Institute, "Bone Cancer: Questions and Answers," page last reviewed March 13, 2008, www.cancer.gov/ cancertopics/factsheet/Sites-Types/bone (accessed March 19, 2010).

10. Juliette Walker, interview with author, September 7, 2008.

11. National Cancer Institute, "Diagnosis," *What You Need to Know about Liver Cancer*, posted April 29, 2009, www.cancer.gov/ cancertopics/wyntk/liver/page6 (accessed December 30, 2009).

12. National Cancer Institute, "Pap Test," page last reviewed February 2, 2009, www.cancer.gov/cancertopics/factsheet/Detection/ Pap-test (accessed December 30, 2009).

13. The Cancer Blog, wap.thecancerblog.com/category/celebrity -spokesperson/ (accessed March 17, 2010).

14. Amber Luchterhand, interview with author, December 4, 2009.

15. U.S. Department of Health and Human Services, National Cancer Institute, and National Institute of Environmental Sciences, *Cancer and the Environment: What You Need to Know*, NIH Publication No. 03–2039, August 2003, www.cancer.gov/images/ Documents/5d17e03e-b39f-4b40-a214-e9e9099c4220/Cancer%20 and%20the%20Environment.pdf (accessed March 19, 2010).

16. Seth Paulson, interview with author, August 26, 2008.

17. National Cancer Institute, "Bone Cancer."

18. National Cancer Institute, "Adolescents and Young Adults with Cancer," www.cancer.gov/cancertopics/aya/types (accessed December 30, 2009).

19. Justin Thomas, interview with author, December 15, 2009.

20. Amanda Nicholls, interview with author, December 13, 2009.

RESOURCES

The National Cancer Institute offers online fact sheets about most types of cancer. This is a good place to start learning about a form of cancer you want to know more about.

www.cancer.gov/cancertopics/factsheet/Sites-Types

Teens Living with Cancer is a great website. This page will tell you what you need to know about specific teen cancers.

www.teenslivingwithcancer.org/cancer-facts/what-is-cancer/

LIVESTRONG, the Lance Armstrong Foundation, is a great place to find answers to all your questions. A good place to start is the "Find More Resources" page.

www.livestrong.org/Get-Help/Find-More-Resources

The LIVESTRONG site can also help you find emotional support.

www.livestrong.org/Get-Help/Find-More-Resources#/f/EmotionalSupport

The LIVESTRONG Cancer Clinical Trial Matching Service may help you find a clinical trial that matches your diagnosis and treatment history.

www.emergingmed.com/networks/livestrong/

Fighting the Good Fight

We have learned a lot about treating cancer, and the best approach involves three tactics: surgery, radiation therapy, and chemotherapy. When an older person gets cancer, the doctors have to take into consideration that the oldster may also have other age-related complications like heart disease, kidney problems, or high blood pressure. But when they are treating someone who is basically young and strong, they can pull out all the stops.

"It allows us to use a combination of those three kinds of treatment up to the point of trying to get rid of all the cancer while just barely not causing irreversible damage to organs," says Dr. Paul Sondel.

It's tough for the kids, and it's tough for the family, but we can be more aggressive in our treatment with a young person in a few ways.

First the regimens themselves can involve stronger doses given on a more frequent basis, and the kids can recover faster. Second, because kids recover faster, we don't need such long delays between treatment that are required for treating adults.

The third is the social thing. A sixteen-year-old cancer patient pretty much sees that the rest of his or her life is dependent on doing everything right with their cancer therapy. As such the cancer treatment takes top priority. We let the child's physiological ability to tolerate the drugs take precedence as we work with the family. We don't delay treatment by two weeks because they have an exam to take.

To be honest, I'm tired of all this mumbo jumbo. I hate chemo. I hate clinic. I hate that the precious little children there have been exposed so often to this medical crap that they can basically hang their own bag of fluids, flush their ports, take their own blood pressure. Two- and three-year-olds shouldn't know how to do these things. I shouldn't even know. But the sad reality is that we do. I'm ready to kick cancer's butt.

—Amber Luchterhand[1]

GOOD READ: *Not Just a Pretty Face* by Stacy Malkan

The author of this book does not paint a pretty picture of the companies that produce the makeup you wear. She is cofounder of Campaign for Safe Cosmetics, and her book exposes the dangers of makeup, baby shampoo, deodorant, and hundreds of other "beauty" products we all use.

Two of the biggest offenders are nail polish and lipstick, and her charges are backed by analysis of blood studies that show the same chemicals in cosmetics turning up throughout the user's body.

Since her book was published, Stacy has visited more than thirty cities to speak about the problem of chemicals in cosmetics.

This book also tells the story of people who are fighting the use of hazardous chemicals in beauty products, including teenage girls who have organized the Teen Safe Cosmetics Campaign. You'll find a chapter on what we can all do to eliminate some of these dangers.

Publisher: Consortium Book Sales & Dist.
Publication Date: 2007
Pages: 192

Their teachers understand that the exam has to wait for the chemotherapy.[2]

Surgery is used to cut out the cancer you can see. Because cancer cells can spread, the tissue around the tumor and nearby lymph nodes may also be removed during the operation. Sometimes radiation or chemotherapy is used first to shrink the tumor. Sometimes arms or legs have to be removed to get at tumors in the bone.

Radiation therapy burns out cancer that doctors can see but can't remove surgically. See the sidebar on radiation therapy for more information.

Chemotherapy is simply poisons used to kill cancer cells. Doctors often use a combination of both radiation and chemotherapy. Learn more in the sidebar on chemotherapy in this chapter.

Research is beginning to show that cancer affects teens and young adults differently than it does kids or older people. The great progress in treating children and older people does not show up when you look at statistics for teens and young adults. That's one reason why doctors are starting to think that teens' bodies react differently to cancer. As your body transitions from child to adult, things are changing fast in there, and researchers are just starting to discover more about how this affects the way teens respond to cancer and cancer treatment.[3]

In the meantime, teens with cancer usually find themselves in the children's hospital or ward because their condition seems closer to the cancers that hit children than those that older people get. Most children's cancer centers treat patients up to the age of twenty, but in some cases doctors may continue to work with their patients when they are older.

THE FIRST BONE MARROW TRANSPLANT EVER WAS PERFORMED ON A TEEN

More than thirty-five years ago, doctors at the University of Minnesota inserted a syringe into David Stahl, a sixteen-year-old suffering from advanced lymphoma, and injected him with disease-fighting bone marrow donated by his little brother.

The procedure (along with chemotherapy) saved the teen's life and was recorded in history as the world's first successful bone marrow transplant for cancer. David is one of many who have received a new lease on life from a bone marrow transplant.

David's family was willing to try the experimental procedure because his prognosis was so grim. Doctors who discovered the grapefruit-sized tumor in his stomach said he had just a 5 percent chance of survival using the standard treatments available in 1975 for lymphoma, which attacks the body's immune system.

Dr. John Kersey, director of the university's cancer center, decided that a transplant was David's best chance. Dr. Kersey believed that clean marrow would give his patient a new, rejuvenated immune system capable of fighting the tumor.

First, David's own diseased marrow was effectively killed off through a course of radiation. Then the transplant from his brother, a perfect match, was carried out. Today, bone marrow transplants like the one performed on David are standard treatment for people with lymphoma and many other forms of cancer and have saved thousands of lives.

Another lasting impact of Dr. Kersey's innovative procedure was that it spurred research into stem cells, the building blocks of the human body. While it wasn't clearly understood at the time, stem cells enable transplant patients to regenerate healthy tissue—and they may hold the key for treating other serious illnesses.[4]

Being grouped with younger children during treatment can create complications for teenagers. "Teens are at the threshold of life, increasingly separating from parents, developing close peer and romantic relationships, and thinking about the future—about things like college and jobs. But when confronted with a life-threatening diagnosis, along with that

☑ DONATING YOUR TISSUE FOR RESEARCH

If you are a cancer patient, you may be asked to provide some of your tissue for medical research. Tissue can include materials from your body such as skin, hair, nails, blood, and urine.

Your tissue may be used in all types of research, such as finding the causes of cancer or other diseases, and developing new tests or new drugs. Research on your tissue along with tissue from others could help researchers learn things that can save lives.

The tissue that you give to research is leftover tissue from medical tests. Doctors usually destroy this unneeded tissue, but you may choose to allow this leftover tissue to be stored and used for future research.

Your tissue cannot be used for research without your written consent, and what you decide will not affect your medical care. However, if you do donate your tissue for research, you will know that you helped researchers as they look for new ways to prevent and treat cancer.[6]

diagnosis comes the need to surrender their growing independence and rely upon their parents once again," says Melissa Carpentier, assistant professor of pediatrics at the Indiana University School of Medicine.

"Unfortunately, teens are often lumped together with children when we consider the psychological effects of cancer, but they differ in many aspects from children and really should be focused on as a distinct group," she says. "We need to take teens' unique perceptions into account and listen to what they are struggling with."[5]

Libby

The biggest problem was the boredom. There aren't usually a lot of other teens on the floor. Doctors sometimes have a problem switching from kid mode to teen mode. They might talk to your parent instead of you. They might talk in a little kid voice. The doctors who really knew you weren't so bad.

I had a laptop that I took with me and played Civilization and The Sims. I would be admitted and go in. I would have my own room with a hospital bed and my side table with my computer and juice and whatever else I had to play with. My mom would sit and read books or watch TV. She was probably a lot more bored than I was.

Chemo made me start to feel nauseous a couple hours after they gave it to me. I also had body sores that were really painful. Chemo is dreadful. But it's a trade-off—you have to do it. It's what you do. I was hooked to an IV [intravenous infusion] and home in bed for a year and a half. At least at home I could work on model boats.[7]

WHAT IS RADIATION THERAPY?

About half of all people with cancer are treated with radiation therapy.

When radiation hits the cancer cells, it damages their genetic material so they can't divide. Radiation therapy tries to damage as many cancer cells as possible without harming many normal cells, but most normal cells can recover from the effects of radiation.

Some types of radiation can penetrate more deeply into the body than others. And some types can be pinpointed at areas as small as an inch of tissue without damaging normal cells nearby.

Radiation therapy can be an external beam, where a machine aims radiation at cancer cells, or it can be internal, where radiation is put inside your body, in or near the cancer cells.

Radiation does not kill cancer cells right away. After days or weeks of treatment, the cancer cells will start to die and keep dying for weeks or months after radiation therapy ends.

Radiation therapy can cause side effects. Your skin may become dry, itch, or peel. You need to take special care of your skin during radiation therapy. You could feel worn out. You could have other side effects, depending on what part of your body is being treated.

Radiation can make your hair fall out because it damages cells that grow quickly, such as cancer cells and the cells in your hair roots. You will only lose hair from radiation therapy on the part of your body being treated, which is different from hair loss from chemotherapy, which happens all over your body.

You may start losing hair two to three weeks after your first radiation therapy. It will take about a week to all fall out. After your radiation treatment is done, your hair may grow back in three to six months. Once your hair grows back, it may look different. It may be thinner or more curly. It may be darker or lighter than it was before.

There is a good link on radiation therapy side effects and ways to manage them in the resources section at the end of this chapter.[8, 9, 10]

Amber

I spent a lot of time in the hospital. It would be three or four weeks at a time, and then I would get out for a couple weeks.

You can always tell someone who is new in the hospital. You can see that they are scared to death. There were times going to the hospital was normal for me. I would go into the waiting room and take my shoes off. Someone new would be all prim and proper, like you were supposed to be. We were messing around with our feet propped up. Cancer isn't a laughing matter, but we had to laugh.

Chapter 2

I started when I was fourteen and did chemo for five years with six months off. I didn't have a normal teenage life, but it was all I knew.

The first two and a half years of treatment were relatively easy. I went into remission after only a month of chemo. They still had to do all the treatment. They have to kill all the cells everywhere. Leukemia has a tendency to hide in the spinal cord. That's what happened to me. It came back in my central nervous system.

When I relapsed, all the treatments were more aggressive. I had a lot of complications. I got a blood clot, and that was the scariest time. I was in the emergency room, and I really thought I was going to die. They told me they were going to put me to sleep. My mom was there, and my dad was trying to get there. Usually I could hide my fear or suppress it. I tried to be strong because I had to be, but moments like that, I was terrified.

The chemo they were giving me was so dangerous to your veins. The treatments are so dangerous that the nurses have gloves up to their arms. It makes you think, "Why are you putting this poison in me when you don't even want to touch it with your own skin?" It was scary.

They put the chemo in through a port, that's a little plastic disc with a line that goes under your skin, and the line from the disc goes into a vein going to your heart. They use it instead of putting a needle in your vein. Anybody who has ever been in the hospital knows that getting IVs really damages your veins. So they use ports for cancer patients who are going to have a lot of treatments.

The side effects of chemo are really bad. I remember infusions they would give me that were a really bright yellow color, and it just looked toxic to me. I was scared of it. Within the first twenty minutes, I would start to feel sick to my stomach.

After seven months of treatment in the hospital, they sent me home with pills. I had to take eighteen pills every six hours—that's seventy-two pills a day. I would have to wake up at midnight to take eighteen pills. It became my life. Chemo. Even just thinking about chemo now makes me feel sick.

At one point, I just didn't want to take all those medications. They were just making me worse—especially the second time. I was torn. I wanted to live. It would be stupid not to try this treatment, but it was so hard.

I'm not saying I was a perfect patient. There are days when you really don't feel good and you have to lay around and feel bad for yourself, but the more you lay around, the worse you feel, and it's a horrible vicious cycle, and it's going to make you feel even worse. My friends in high school had other things going on. I felt left out, and at first I spent all the time in the hospital bed staring at the walls and watching TV.

The hospital had activities, but since I was a teenager and it was a children's hospital, I didn't interact with a lot of them at first. Towards the end of my treatment I started to come out of my room more and spend time with the nurses. That inspired me to be a nurse, seeing what they do. I started to make more friends with the other patients. They were younger than me, but we were going through the same thing.

If your doctor will let you out of your room—get out! It's not good to spend all your time alone. It makes you feel worse to be thinking about how sick you are. I found myself thinking too much when I was alone. It always felt better when I was out doing something.[11]

* * *

EXERCISE AND CANCER—GET PHYSICAL

While going through chemotherapy and other cancer treatments, the last thing you may feel like doing is exercising, but according to the American Cancer Society, mild exercise can really help you get back in the game. Some studies show that going too easy on yourself while wiped out by the fatigue that chemotherapy, radiation therapy, and surgery can cause may actually make you weaker. Ask your doctor how quickly you can start exercising again, and go for it.[12]

Also, once you have been diagnosed with cancer, you are more likely to get cancer again. Research is constantly coming up

FIVE FUN WAYS TO PREVENT CANCER WITH EXERCISE

Dancing

Dancing is a great way to work up a sweat. You can do it in your own room, or you can do it with friends. Maybe you can get some buddies to take a Latin dance class with you or get into hip-hop.

Rollerblading

This is great exercise. It is a good cardiovascular workout, and works just about every muscle in your body. But you have to be careful that you don't end up with injuries. That would not accomplish your exercise goal. Be sure you wear the proper protective gear, like a helmet, and knee and elbow pads.

Join a Team Sport

See what your school has to offer and don't forget your local recreation center. Joining a team is good exercise and gets you together with other people who are also into exercise.

Swimming

Swimming is another one of those exercises that is both a good cardiovascular workout and puts all your muscles through their paces. Find out what hours area pools are open for free swim and dive in.

Cycling

Cycling is a way to enjoy a little sightseeing while you exercise. Get your bike out of the garage, pick a pretty area in your neighborhood, and get moving.

with more reasons why exercise is good for you. You've heard a lot of them already. Preventing cancer is at the top of the list.

What is important here is that physical activity has been shown to give you some protection against many forms of cancer. Prevention of cancers of the colon, breast, prostate, lung, and uterus have all been linked to exercise. Exercise can also increase your energy, improve your mood, boost your self-esteem, and stimulate your immune system. What's not to like?[13]

Exactly how exercise protects you is not completely understood yet. Obviously exercise can reduce obesity, which has been related to some cancers. It can also change body hormones, which may do something good. By speeding up your metabolism, exercise just moves food through your system faster, and if you have eaten something toxic, it may not hang around long enough to do damage.[14]

So how much exercise do you need? The American Cancer Society says you need to exercise at least five days a week for at least thirty minutes a day, which can be broken into ten-minute segments. That's enough to make a difference in how you look and how you feel, and hopefully help protect you from another cancer.

There are times when you want to assert your independence and function on your own. You know that cancer treatment is your number one priority in order to live the rest of your life, but on a daily basis you hate it and don't want to participate. That's the time to reach out to your team. Maybe it's your doctor or nurse, social worker, or psychologist—you need to let them know how you feel. They are there to help you. Your

NICOLE KIDMAN FIGHTS CANCER

When Nicole Kidman was seventeen, her mother was diagnosed with breast cancer; Nicole has also lost friends to breast cancer. Nicole's parents are Australian, but she was born in Hawaii, so she has dual citizenship in Australia and the United States. She has worked all over the world on women's health issues, including cancer.

As a teen, Nicole's first love was ballet, but she switched to acting and broke into movies at the age of sixteen. When her mother was diagnosed with cancer, Nicole stopped working and took a massage course so that she could help her mom with physical therapy. Her mother survived the cancer.[15]

Nicole has put her celebrity to good use, focusing attention on cancer research by becoming the first ambassador for the Women's Cancer Research Fund in Great Britain. She has received Australia's highest civilian honor for "service to the performing arts as an acclaimed motion picture performer, to health care through contributions to improve medical treatment for women and children and advocacy for cancer research."

"Together we will beat cancer," Nicole says.[16]

WHAT IS CHEMOTHERAPY?

The good news is that chemotherapy can stop or slow the dangerously fast growth and division of cancer cells. The bad news is that chemotherapy also goes after healthy cells that divide quickly, such as the cells that line your mouth and intestines and that cause your hair to grow.

You may need to stay in the hospital during chemotherapy, or you may be treated in a doctor's office and then go home. Chemotherapy is given in many ways.

Injection: Chemotherapy can be given as a shot.
Intra-arterial: It can be injected into an artery that is feeding the cancer.
Intraperitoneal: It can go directly into the peritoneal cavity—the area that contains your intestines, stomach, liver, and ovaries.
Intravenous: It can go directly into a vein.
Topically: Chemotherapy comes in a cream that you rub onto your skin.
Orally: Chemotherapy comes in pills, capsules, or liquids that you swallow.

Side Effects of Chemotherapy

The list of possible side effects from chemotherapy is long. Luckily not everyone gets every side effect. There is a good link to learn about side effects and how to deal with them at the end of this chapter in the resources section.

When chemotherapy damages healthy cells in your body, you experience side effects. Often side effects get better or go away after chemotherapy is over, but research is starting to discover late effects from some treatments. Ask your doctor what you should be on the look out for from your particular type of chemotherapy.[17]

social worker may go to your doctor and ask to tweak your treatment. Don't forget your teachers and friends. There is someone who can help you through this.

Juliette

My kind of chemo was quite the ordeal. I would have to stay in my room, and the nurse would come in wearing a special blue gown so if the chemo spilled, she wouldn't get it on her skin. It took three hours. They would do it at night so I was in bed.

When I was in the hospital, I got really sick and threw up a lot. I got very, very weak. Usually I'm really strong because I'm an athlete, but I lost a lot of weight and was tired all the time.

GOOD FILM: *Cancer Warrior*

This is a sixty-minute film that was shown on television, and you can watch it online at www.pbs.org/wgbh/nova/cancer/program.html.

Join Dr. Judah Folkman as he shares his forty-year quest for a radically new cancer treatment, including the development of the much-touted drug Endostatin. As a young doctor, Dr. Folkman proposed that a tumor could not grow to be life-threatening if the blood supply to it were blocked.

Focusing on the blood vessels that feed tumors rather than the cancer itself, he and his colleagues have made giant steps toward starving the bad cells while keeping the rest of the body healthy. In this film, Folkman invites cameras into his lab for a first-person look at the groundbreaking clinical research that offers hope to cancer patients.

This is a clear, compelling story of a dedicated scientist and a radical new way to treat cancer.

It was really hard to see myself look that weak. I got through it because I knew I only had three months of it, and then I could get back to everything.

It was hard to deal with the side effects. I got really sick, and I would get blisters on my feet. My body would ache, and I would get really sore. I had to be very careful because if I got a fever, or something went wrong, I would have to go back into the hospital.

When I was in the hospital, I felt isolated from the outside world. I remember it would get lonely up there sometimes. I had some friends come by, and when the kids were playing in the halls and play rooms, it would be all right. The little kids running around definitely helped take your mind off things.[18]

Seth

I was introduced to the doctor, and he seemed like a really nice guy from the get-go. He explained the situation of how many treatments of chemo and radiation I would be going through. Then he talked to me on a one-to-one basis, and told me that my cancer was a fast cancer. I had B-cell large diffuse lymphoma. It was very treatable.

For me, chemo wasn't as bad as radiation. The chemo made me tired. I had chemo every other day. Each treatment took at least half a day. I used to watch movies. That made it go faster.

Then I had twenty rounds of radiation. They put permanent tattoos on my chest—little dots to aim the beam. I had a treatment every day. I always got dehydrated. I hated the medication I took for radiation. It had a bitter taste.

Seth and his physician, Dr. Brad Kahl. *Courtesy of Seth Paulson.*

Since the cancer was in my chest, the radiation came close to my throat, and the deeper radiation caused my throat to contract. It was a side effect. They warned me before, but I didn't think it would be as bad as it was. I could only eat yogurt and apple sauce, things like that. Radiation could wipe me out for the day.

And when we started to get sunny days in spring, I had to stay out of the sun because radiation made me vulnerable to skin cancer. That was the hardest part.

I go in for a check-up every three months now. I go in for blood work and a CT scan. Then my doctor tells me the results. He tells me that everything is fine. I do wonder when I go in, is there a chance the cancer could be back.

THE U.S. NATIONAL CANCER INSTITUTE IS WORKING FOR YOU

The U.S. National Cancer Institute (NCI) is a great source of hope for curing cancer. It is one of many organizations working toward this goal, but it is also one of the biggest. In 2008, it sent almost 5 billion dollars out to support cancer research in universities, medical schools, cancer centers, research labs, and private firms in the United States and sixty other countries around the world to speed cancer research toward the cures everyone is waiting for.

NCI has built a national network that includes regional and community cancer centers, physicians who are cancer specialists, groups of clinical researchers and community outreach groups. Their goal is to support promising research projects on the causes, diagnosis, treatment, and prevention of cancer.

One of their biggest jobs is making sure that cancer patients and the public understand what they can do to reduce their risk of cancer, understand about the importance of early detection of cancer, and help anyone diagnosed with cancer.

Because of the work of NCI scientists and cancer researchers throughout the United States and the rest of the world, real progress is being made against cancer. People with cancer are living longer and have a better quality of life than ever before. In 2008, there were more than 11 million cancer survivors in the United States.

You can learn more about cancer at the NCI website. They have a entire section dedicated to cancers that affect teens.[19]

I'm healthy now. Every time I go in for a check, and it's good, that makes my day.[20]

Justin

I ended up staying in the hospital for a whole week, and they started me on treatment and put me on an eight-month program to phase out my chemo. They removed my spleen in August, two months later. I went through three surgeries.

Because I'm an active person, being in bed all day is not my style. I hated being constricted. I love to move. I was supposed to stay in bed because I was getting a spinal tap. But I couldn't stay there. The nurse was always looking for me because I was always out of my bed.[21]

*   *   *

CLINICAL TRIALS—ARE THEY FOR YOU?

Clinical trials are research studies that test how well new medical approaches work in people. They answer scientific questions and try to find better ways to prevent, screen for, diagnose, or treat a disease. If you take part in a cancer clinical trial, you have an opportunity to add to the knowledge doctors use to fight cancer. Because there has been less research done on teens and young adults with cancer, this is an opportunity to add to research that can help other teens.[22]

Trials test types of treatments such as new drugs, new approaches to surgery or radiation therapy, or new combinations of treatments. Some trials explore ways to make you more comfortable during treatment. Researchers may be looking at ways to help people who are going through nausea, sleep problems, depression, and other effects of cancer or its treatment.

Dr. Paul Sondel is a professor of pediatrics, human oncology, and medical genetics at the University of Wisconsin–Madison. He is also a member of the Children's Oncology Group, a national team of clinical researchers working together to come up with better answers. Some clinical tests cover rare situations. According to Dr. Sondel,

If you tried to test something like an engineered protein just here in Madison, Wisconsin, it might take ten years to get eight patients who were eligible for that test. But by doing it at the national level, we can test patients from all around the country. Virtually every type of child's cancer is part of this consortium.

We are not basing treatment on what was published in last month's medical journals. That information was submitted six months ago based on data that was collected two years ago. We are basing treatment on real-time data analysis through the Children's Oncology Group.[23]

A group of doctors, researchers, and community leaders watches as clinical trials are conducted to make sure the study is fair and participants are not likely to be harmed. This group can stop a trial if it appears to be causing unexpected harm to the participants. And the group can also stop a clinical trial if there is clear evidence that the new intervention is effective so that everyone who needs it can benefit, not just those in the trial.

Sometimes health insurance providers will not cover the cost of a clinical trial, if they consider the approach being tested to be experimental. It may help to have someone from the research team talk to your insurance company.

The bad news is that new drugs and procedures are not always better than the standard care. New treatments may have side effects that are worse than those you would experience in standard care. You may not be able to choose the kind of treatment you receive, and you may have to visit the doctor more often than in standard care.

The good news is that if you are in a clinical trial, you have access to promising new approaches that are often not available outside the trial. If the method being tested is successful, you will be one of the first to benefit. You will also know that the trial will be helping others in the future.[24]

Peter

I was treated in the children's wing because osteosarcoma is a common type of cancer in children. The summer after the cancer was diagnosed, [every three or four weeks] I was in the hospital for about a week for chemotherapy. Then they did a knee replacement. They put in a metal joint, and I had chemotherapy for the rest of the fall, and that was supposed to take care of it.

I was done with treatment and in remission for a while, but the next summer the cancer came back in my knee. I had moved to Milwaukee and was going to college there. I started to have pain in my lungs. I would be walking home, and I could hardly breathe. The bone cells were duplicating more than they needed to. It started on the outside of the left femur and from there it spread to my lungs. I also had lymph nodes taken out that came back with cancer as well. My oncologist said, "Losing your leg is your best chance now." That was the easiest hard decision I've ever had to make.

But every time the cancer came back, that stabbed me through the heart. I'd go for a scan, and then get a home call, and it was like, something is in your blood again. It was back, and they would do more surgery.

That's when I had to find a lot of hobbies to keep myself busy and at least somewhat sane. Music. I started writing songs, and I did a lot of painting. I had a fascination with painting. I never had any training. I just did it. I had my own style.

In the old children's hospital from most of the windows all you could see was more of the hospital. I would switch rooms to try to get a view of a tree. I painted a lot of birds. It always felt good to see a bird. It's a simple life. The bird doesn't know about cancer. They are just birds thinking about worms. I wanted to be a bird.[25]

* * *

ACUPUNCTURE: AN ANCIENT METHOD GETS A NEW TWIST

Acupuncture applies needles, heat, pressure, and other treatments to certain places on the skin as a form of healing. It is part of a medical system that has been used in China for thousands of years to prevent, diagnose, and treat disease.

People who use acupuncture believe that chi, a form of vital energy, flows through our bodies along a network of paths, called meridians. Chi has two forces, yin and yang, which are opposites that work together to form a whole. If your yin and yang are not in balance, chi can become blocked, and this blockage causes pain, illness, and other health problems. Traditional Chinese medicine uses acupuncture, diet, herbal therapy, meditation, physical exercise, and massage to restore health by unblocking chi and rebalancing your yin and yang.

The U.S. Food and Drug Administration approved the acupuncture needle as a medical device in 1996. Many illnesses are treated with acupuncture, but it is mainly used to control pain, including pain in cancer patients. It is usually used in addition to conventional cancer therapy.

We usually think of needles when we think of acupuncture. These are disposable, stainless steel needles that are slightly thicker than a human hair. The acupuncture practitioner decides where to insert the needles based on the problem being treated. Once the needles are inserted, they may be twirled, moved up and down at different speeds, heated, or charged with a weak electric current.

There have been scientific studies on using acupuncture to treat cancer and its side effects. In some studies, acupuncture helped lower the pain cancer patients were feeling. Sometimes patients have been able to take less or even no drugs for pain while using acupuncture, but more tests are needed to be sure.

Other tests have shown that acupuncture can help relieve nausea and vomiting cased by chemotherapy. Clinical trials are studying the effects of acupuncture on cancer and symptoms caused by cancer treatment, including weight loss, cough, chest pain, fever, anxiety, depression, and fluid in the arms or legs. Studies have shown that, for many patients, treatment with acupuncture either relieves symptoms or keeps them from getting worse.

Sometimes people have experienced complications from acupuncture. Because other cancer treatments such as chemotherapy and radiation therapy weaken your immune system, if the needles are not completely free of germs, they can cause infection. Other patients report feeling soreness and pain, lightheaded, or sleepy during the treatment. It is important to work with a qualified acupuncture practitioner who uses a new set of disposable (single-use) needles.[26]

⊚⊚⊚⊚⊚⊚⊚⊚⊚⊚⊚⊚⊚⊚⊚⊚⊚⊚

ALTERNATIVE MEDICINE

In 2008, as many as 80 million people in the United States used some form of alternative medicine, from herbs to megavitamins to yoga and acupuncture. Some of these alternatives make great claims, but the scientific evidence isn't there in most cases.[27] Complementary and alternative medicine is treatment that is not considered part of conventional, or usual, cancer treatment. Some alternatives may be helpful, but it is important to work with your doctor or nurse to make sure alternative treatments are not interfering with the treatment your doctor is using.

It is important to test alternative medicine the same way conventional treatments are tested, and the NCI is funding a number of clinical trials at medical centers to evaluate alternative therapies for cancer.

Some alternative therapies are being accepted by conventional medicine—not as cures, but as complementary therapies than can help patients feel better and recover faster. For example, acupuncture (the technique of inserting thin needles through the skin at specific points on the body to control pain and other symptoms) has been found to help with chemotherapy-caused nausea and vomiting, and also in controlling pain from surgery.[28]

However, tests have also shown that some alternative treatments don't work and could make you sicker. Always run any ideas you hear about medical treatments past your current doctor.

Many young cancer survivors decide to pursue careers in medicine because of the positive aspects of their time in treatment. They are taking what they learned about the world and about themselves during their battles with cancer and using those skills to step into adulthood.

Amber Luchterhand found her career goal during treatment. "I started college in August, and I hope to get into the nursing program," she says. "It's not only a good job for me, but a way I can help people. I want to give back to the nursing field because of everything that I've been through. Some of my nurses who treated me had been through the cancer thing, and it was cool to talk to them and hear their success stories."

Amber continues, "I've been around the medical field so much that it comes pretty easy to me. Right now I'm taking anatomy and physiology, and I'm doing really well."[29]

Juliette Walker agrees. "I'm not really sure what major I want to do, but after going through all this stuff at the hospital, it kind of makes me want to see about a career in medicine. All the nurses that I had—I really loved them. They seem to really love what they are doing. I'm not sure about being a doctor, but all the doctors too were very compassionate and had a passion for what they were doing. It would be rewarding to be able to help people the way they helped me."[30]

NOTES

1. Amber Luchterhand, hospital journal.

2. Dr. Paul M. Sondel, professor of pediatrics, human oncology, and medical genetics, University of Wisconsin–Madison, interview with author, July 1, 2008.

3. Archie Bleyer, Ronald Barr, Brandon Hayes-Lattin, and David Thomas, "The Distinctive Biology of Cancer in Adolescents and Young Adults," *Nature Reviews Cancer* 8 (April 1, 2008): 297. Roni Caryn Rabin, "In Cancer Fight, Teenagers Don't Fit In," *New York Times*, Health section, March 15, 2010, www.nytimes.com/2010/03/16/health/16canc.html?hp (accessed March 17, 2010).

4. Nicole Endres, "30 Years of Hope," UM News, March 7, 2006, www1.umn.edu/news/features/2006/UR_87495_REGION1.html (accessed December 7, 2010).

5. Indiana University News Room, "Teens with Cancer Present Unique Psychological Issues," Indiana University, newsinfo.iu.edu/news/page/normal/10457.html (accessed December 30, 2009).

6. National Cancer Institute, "Providing Your Tissue for Research: What You Need to Know," posted February 2, 2006, www.cancer.gov/clinicaltrials/resources/providingtissue (accessed March 19, 2010).

7. Libby Falck, interview with author, July 11, 2008.

8. National Cancer Institute, "Radiation Therapy for Cancer," reviewed June 30, 2010, www.cancer.gov/cancertopics/factsheet/Therapy/radiation (accessed December 7, 2010).

9. National Cancer Institute, "Questions and Answers about Radiation Therapy," *Radiation Therapy and You: Support for People*

with Cancer, posted April 20, 2007, www.cancer.gov/cancertopics/radiation-therapy-and-you/page2 (accessed December 30, 2009).

10. National Cancer Institute, "Radiation Therapy Side Effects and Ways to Manage Them," *Radiation Therapy and You: Support for People with Cancer*, posted April 20, 2007, www.cancer.gov/cancertopics/radiation-therapy-and-you/page8#SE4 (accessed December 30, 2009).

11. Amber Luchterhand, interview with author, December 4, 2009.

12. American Cancer Society, "Exercise Key to Improved Quality of Life for Cancer Patients," ww3.cancer.org/docroot/MIT/content/MIT_2_4X_Exercise_Key_To_Improved_Quality_of_Life_for_Cancer_Patients.asp?sitearea=MIT (accessed March 19, 2010).

13. National Children's Cancer Society, *The Mountain You Have Climbed: A Young Adult's Guide to Childhood Cancer Survivorship: Beyond the Cure*, www.nationalchildrenscancersociety.org/NetCommunity/Document.Doc?id=51 (accessed March 19, 2010).

14. University of Iowa Hospitals and Clinics, "Exercise and Cancer Prevention," last revised April 2003, www.uihealthcare.com/topics/medicaldepartments/cancercenter/cancertips/exercise.html (accessed March 19, 2010).

15. Internet Movie Database, "Biography for Nicole Kidman," www.imdb.com/name/nm0000173/bio (accessed March 19, 2010).

16. Look to the Stars, "Nicole Kidman's Charity Work, Events and Causes," www.looktothestars.org/celebrity/185-nicole-kidman (accessed March 19, 2010).

17. National Cancer Institute, "Questions and Answers about Chemotherapy," *Chemotherapy and You: Support for People with Cancer*, posted June 29, 2007, www.cancer.gov/cancertopics/chemotherapy-and-you/page2 (accessed December 30, 2009).

18. Juliette Walker, interview with author, September 7, 2008.

19. National Cancer Institute, "The U.S. National Cancer Institute," reviewed July 23, 2010, www.cancer.gov/cancertopics/factsheet/NCI/NCI (accessed December 7, 2010).

20. Seth Paulson, interview with author, August 26, 2008.

21. Justin Thomas, interview with author, December 15, 2009.

22. Bleyer et al., "The Distinctive Biology of Cancer in Adolescents and Young Adults," 288.

23. Sondel, interview.

24. National Cancer Institute, "Cancer Clinical Trials," reviewed April 27, 2010, www.cancer.gov/cancertopics/factsheet/Information/clinical-trials (accessed December 7, 2010).

25. Peter Greenwood, interview with author, August 11, 2008.

26. National Cancer Institute, "Acupuncture," modified March 5, 2010, www.cancer.gov/cancertopics/pdq/cam/acupuncture/ patient/45.cdr#Section_45 (accessed March 24, 2010).

27. William J. Broad, "Applying Science to Alternative Medicine," *New York Times*, Health section, September 29, 2008, www.nytimes .com/2008/09/30/health/research/30tria.html?_r=1&ref=health (accessed December 30, 2009).

28. National Cancer Institute, "Complementary and Alternative Medicine in Cancer Treatment," last modified November 16, 2009, www.cancer.gov/cancertopics/pdq/cam/cam-cancer-treatment/ patient/allpages (accessed December 30, 2009).

29. Luchterhand, interview.

30. Walker, interview.

RESOURCES

Cancer.Net has a great page on managing side effects. You can find the facts on everything from appetite loss to sleeping problems to weight gain. Much of the information here is used to teach doctors about side effects. It is very complete.

www.cancer.net/patient/All+About+Cancer/Treating+Cancer/ Managing+Side+Effects

Teens Living with Cancer can share firsthand experiences on what to expect.

www.teenslivingwithcancer.org/cancer-facts/treatment/

TeensHealth has firsthand descriptions of chemotherapy, radiation therapy, and what it's like to have surgery.

kidshealth.org/teen/diseases_conditions/cancer/chemo.html

The NCI website is a good place to learn about side effects of chemotherapy and how to deal with them.

www.cancer.gov/cancertopics/chemotherapy-and-you/ page7#SE4

The NCI website also has information about side effects of radiation therapy and how you can deal with them.

www.cancer.gov/cancertopics/radiation-therapy-and-you/page8

Eva Vertes has been researching cancer as a teen since 2003. She was only nineteen when she gave this talk discussing her journey toward studying medicine and her drive to understand the roots of cancer and other diseases. She may not have the answers yet, but she is asking some powerful questions. Checkout this video at TED Ideas Worth Spreading.

www.ted.com/talks/lang/eng/eva_vertes_looks_to_the_future_of_medicine.html

You can learn about radiation treatments with this online video from Starlight Foundation called *Welcome to the Radiation Center*.

radiology.starlightprograms.org/

Check out this online video about IVs. Learn about why you need an IV, what it feels like to get one, and how to make it go a little easier.

radiology.starlightprograms.org/

The Family Room

When one person in a family gets diagnosed with cancer, the whole family takes the hit. If you are a teen with cancer, you may be looking at your family differently now.

FEELINGS OF HELPLESSNESS

Cancer can push a teen back into feeling like a helpless baby. Just at the time when you are ready to step away from your family, you need them more than ever before. And just when you need them, they are coping with your cancer, and they are scared and hurting too.

You are fighting for your life, and one of your weapons is the double-edged sword of how you feel about your family members, and how they feel about you.

Sometimes you want your parents to leave you alone, but you don't really want them to leave you alone. You want your family there, but you don't want to be bugged. You don't want them asking, "Are you okay?" "Did you have a bowel movement?"

They feel helpless and are just trying to keep you safe, but if you need time alone, tell them so. The more you take responsibility for your health, the more you can ask them to back off, but be prepared to compromise.

Cancer hits a family like an earthquake off the Richter scale. "So many families are barely holding it together, and then this happens," says Dr. Carol Diamond, associate professor, School

I've seen what cancer can do to a family and a whole community, really. Sometimes it's good, and sometimes it's bad.

—Amber Luchterhand[1]

My dad is no longer in my life. Most of my family is just, "Oh, really? I didn't know you had that." They don't really support me much. My mom takes me to all my doctor appointments. My mom is there for me most of the time, but she has enough stress on her own.

—Amanda Nicholls[3]

of Medicine and Public Health, University of Wisconsin–Madison. "Sometimes it inspires people to do amazing things, and that's quite amazing to see. It can also tear families apart. Either way, it's really hard on teenagers."[2]

YOUR FIRST LINE OF DEFENSE

Your parents can be your A Team, but coaching your mom or dad can be a strange, new position to play. What you need from them can change from day to day or even minute to minute. Try to let them know. Do you need help with your medication? Do you need a hug? Do you need more time with your friends? Do you want them there when you are sick to your stomach? Do you want help talking to the doctor or your teachers?

GOOD READ: *Angels Watching over Me* by Lurlene McDaniel

Sixteen-year-old Leah Lewis-Hall is spending her Christmas in an Indianapolis hospital while her mother is thousands of miles away on a honeymoon with husband number five. Though Leah went to the doctor for only a broken finger, he ordered tests, and now she is trapped in the hospital.

Those tests reveal that Leah has bone cancer, and she deals with her frightening news by turning to her hospital roommate, a young Amish girl named Rebekah, and her big family. A close and loving family is a new experience for Leah.

The plot thickens as Leah finds herself drawn to Ethan, a handsome Amish boy, while her nurse Gabriella may or may not be an angel. The *School Library Journal* says this book has strong religious themes, but avoids being preachy.

Angels Watching over Me won a RITA award, presented by the Romance Writers of America to the best novels in romantic fiction in its teen romance category. The plot has been called fast paced and unexpected. So if you want to know more about dealing with cancer, religious inspiration, or cross-cultural romance, this could be a good read for you.

Publisher: Laurel Leaf
Publication Date: 1996
Pages: 192

Peter

I had just been out on my own, and it wasn't easy to move back home because of the cancer. But home was where I had to be. I have a really big family—seven kids. Most of them are older than me. Between them all, there was somebody there. There was always a sibling around to keep me company. My mom was there at every appointment and bringing me food in the hospital. I wouldn't have gotten through this without them.

Everybody was there in different ways. One brother might stay overnight in the hospital with me. Another brother would come by for an hour. I was just glad to have people around. It's hard getting through treatment. Having family and friends around is one of the most important things. You don't want to sit there by yourself and just think about what you have to deal with. You have enough time to do that.[4]

* * *

NO ONE EXPECTS YOU TO APOLOGIZE FOR HAVING CANCER

You may feel your parents' pain. You can feel guilty because you got cancer, and it is affecting everyone around you. It's important to remember that you are not responsible for your parents' marriage. There are people who can help you if you are worried about your family. Reach out to your nurse or your teacher. Perhaps there is someone in your church or other organization that you belong to who can help you.

Juliette

I felt like a baby the whole time. If anything went wrong, I had to call the doctor or go to the hospital, and because I was in the hospital, I really liked having my mom there during the night. Even though, as a teen, you feel like you should be more independent, I felt like I needed someone there.

BONE MARROW OR STEM CELL TRANSPLANT

If your brother or sister has a cancer such as leukemia, he or she may need a bone marrow transplant. Bone marrow is the soft, sponge-like material inside our bones. It contains immature cells that turn into blood cells. These immature cells can be used for transplants. After the cancer patient's cells have all been destroyed by high doses of radiation and potent chemotherapy, a transplant can restore the cells that produce blood.

To minimize side effects, doctors need to use transplanted cells that match the patient's own cells as closely as possible. Close relatives, especially brothers and sisters, are usually the best match.

If you are a good match and donate bone marrow, you will be either put to sleep or numbed in the area below the waist. Needles are inserted into your pelvic (hip) bone, and the marrow is drawn out in a process called harvesting, which takes about an hour.

I was a bone marrow donor for my brother, and it was not a big deal. The tiny incisions healed quickly, and within a few weeks my body had replaced all the marrow I donated. Some people are back to their usual routine in a few days.

Your brother or sister will receive the donated marrow through an IV line just like a blood transfusion. It will take from one to five hours. After entering the bloodstream, the cells travel to the bone marrow and begin to produce new blood cells. That can take two to four weeks. However, it takes much longer for your brother or sister to build up his or her immune system again. During that time a bone marrow recipient has to be extremely careful about being exposed to germs of any kind.[5]

Just before I was diagnosed, my dad was offered a job in another state. But I changed our plans. We stayed here. My mom had to work just part time, and she stopped working at all during the time I had chemo—to take care of me, I guess.

The worst part—well, there were really two hard parts— the physical part was how sick I got. The medication that was supposed to make me well actually made me so nauseated. The second part was the emotional part of having to kind of make my family go through it with me. I knew they were supporting me, but it was hard watching my friends and family feel sad about what I was going through.[6]

Amber

Our family was never really well off. We always made it, but when I got sick, my mom quit her job to be with me. We didn't know how we were going to pay the bills. We were proud and didn't want anyone to know that we weren't making it.

When I got sick, my whole community pulled together. Every year my school took donations and bought things for my sister and me for Christmas. Our church really helped out. When I was in the hospital, they brought meals to my family.

I had times when I wouldn't let my family know I was struggling physically. But it's important to let people know when you need help.[7]

* * *

WHAT IF YOUR MOM OR DAD HAS CANCER?

It wasn't that long ago your parents were carrying you on their shoulders. When they tell you they have cancer, it may feel like your roles have been reversed. Maybe you feel scared. Maybe you feel angry. Maybe you feel both. People react to learning their parents have cancer in lots of different ways, but there are ways to deal with all your feelings.

It's important to talk with family and friends about what you feel. You may also want to write your thoughts in a journal. There are support groups and counselors out there who can help you through the experience. Look around to see who you can ask for help. Consider aunts, uncles, grandparents, teachers, coaches, school nurses, social workers, troop leaders, pastors, rabbis, and priests. Give it some thought. Who can support you?

No matter how much help your family gets, you will probably need to take more responsibility than other kids your age. You may be doing more chores such as making dinner and doing the laundry. You may have to look after younger brothers and sisters. You may be spending more time home alone. There is an upside here. You will learn a lot from the

Chelsea and Chase with their mom, cancer survivor Connie. *Courtesy of Chase and Chelsea Prochnow.*

experience and be better prepared for the next phase of your life when you grow up and leave home.

Chelsea

When I was eighteen, my mom was diagnosed with breast cancer, and when I was twenty she was diagnosed with leukemia. To be honest, I was never really afraid. I don't know if I just didn't understand the severity of her illness or because my mom was never afraid either. She was very positive through it all.

She had not been feeling well, and even though she is a very high-energy person, she was coming home from work to nap during her lunch. My aunt said she needed to get this checked out. Then my brother called me at school to tell me Mom was in the ER.

That night my parents told Chase and me that they wanted to keep her in the hospital to run more tests. The next day I remember walking into the hospital after classes and both my parents were still at the hospital. They had already moved her into the room where she would spend the next three months of her life. They told me she had cancer.

After that I was at the hospital almost every day. It was a weird thing. The roles were reversed. I was taking care of both my parents. My mom because she wasn't able to do some things, and my dad because he wasn't emotionally stable. He was exhausted because he still worked a full day and was taking care of my mom and worrying about her.

At such a young age I wasn't expecting to be taking care of my parents. But it was something I wanted to do, and it brought us all closer.

Sometimes it was hard to deal with my friends. I felt like nobody understood me. I would try to express what I was feeling to my friends, and they had no idea of what I was going through. I was never afraid, but I was in a whirlwind. I didn't know how to manage everything.

One of the hardest things at first was all the calls I had to take. Family and friends of family would call and say, "How is your mom?" and they would express all their fears and sadness. It was like—you can't do that to me! This was my mom lying in that hospital bed. I felt weighed down with other people's stress and anxiety and fears and all that. They kept calling—family friends who I didn't see on a regular basis, but they had my number.

The hospital offered Care Pages to its long-term patients, which is kind of a blog where you can update family and friends about what is going on. That was a relief for me. It let people keep in touch without weighing on me.

I never went into my mom's room and felt sad or heavy or any emotion except happiness. The more people you are surrounded with who are positive, the better your outcome is going to be.[8]

* * *

To keep from getting snowed under, look for ways to keep things simple. A family calendar can make things go more smoothly and help everyone. You can take charge of keeping it up-to-date. Make a list of what needs to be done, and put the most important things on top. This is a skill you will use all your life.

Try to get as much school work done during school hours as you can. Keep everyone in your life up-to-date with the

TV DOCTOR PATRICK DEMPSEY FIGHTS CANCER

Patrick Dempsey, known by fans of the hit ABC series *Grey's Anatomy* as Dr. Derek Shepherd (or as Dr. McDreamy), also has a dream. He wants everyone who is dealing with cancer to understand their condition and their options, and he has created the Patrick Dempsey Center for Cancer Hope & Healing to make that dream come true.

Though Patrick plays a hard-charging surgeon who can cope with anything on television, he felt as helpless as anyone does when a loved one has cancer. For Patrick, it was his mother, who was diagnosed with ovarian cancer.

"I found out how important it is to have access to good, reliable resources to help the patient, family members, and caretakers," he says. After helping his mother cope with a cancer that returned twice, Patrick says, "I knew that I wanted to make a difference, to give back to the community that helped my mom through her cancer journey."[9] His website does just that.

The center has a home base as part of the Central Maine Comprehensive Cancer Center, but you don't have to live in Maine to take advantage of it. A toll-free Cancer Assistance Line can give you information about local, state, and national resources and services for people living with cancer. You can reach this help by calling 1-877-336-7287.

Not surprisingly for someone who has excelled in television, Patrick Dempsey's website has a Cancer Video Atlas where you can access fifty animated videos on cancer-related topics. The site lets you personalize and search by cancer type, diagnostic test, side effect, or treatment. There is a lot to learn here. His site also includes a link to search for clinical trials that might be appropriate to the cancer in your life. You can connect to the Patrick Dempsey Center for Cancer Hope & Healing through Facebook, Twitter, and YouTube.[10]

situation. Teachers aren't mind readers. Let them know what is happening at home. Talk to your teachers immediately, if you feel like you are falling behind.

Chase

I was eighteen when my mom had cancer. I was sad. I could see that my dad was scared. He had lost his mother to leukemia, but I just had a feeling that she was going to make it.

It was different in our home. Our family friends and members of our church helped out a lot. We had tons of food brought over. It was like they thought me and my dad didn't know how to cook. My football team supported me too. I had a close group of friends that I held tight to.

I did have to take a lot of responsibility for myself. I think it made me grow up faster. It gave both me and Chelsea a lot of responsibility at a young age. The sobering reality of death forces you to grow up right then.

My mother was out of the house, and so was my dad. He was at the hospital a lot. He lost his focus on parenting, but since I was older, I could just keep going to school and playing sports and doing what I always did. I think it's important to cling to the things that you are close to at such times. Surround yourself with your friends and family who care for you.[11]

*   *   *

Though you may think you can take care of everything by yourself, remember that even adults need help when there is a serious illness in the family. You can find places to reach out for help at the end of this chapter.

WHEN YOUR BROTHER OR SISTER HAS CANCER

When you learn that your brother or sister has cancer, you may feel a roaring in your ears. It might be the sound of your own mixed emotions of fear, anger, guilt, sadness, and confusion, or it might be the sound of a vacuum forming around you as

GOOD FILM: *My Sister's Keeper*

My Sister's Keeper is a powerful movie about love and betrayal. It is a winner of the Teen Choice Awards organized by *Teen People* magazine.[12]

Anna, eleven, is played by Abigail Breslin. Her parents decided to have her so she would be a genetic match for her older sister, Kate (played by Sofia Vassilieva), who is suffering from leukemia.

Anna comes to feel that her life is not her own. All of her life choices are dictated by what Kate needs. Then Kate goes into kidney failure. Though Anna was born to donate whatever her sister needs, including a kidney, she decides to fight for the rights to her own body.

Sofia shaved her hair and eyebrows off in order to play the role. She said it was the least she could do to understand Kate's pain. Sofia was filming a TV show at the same time she was making this film, so her long hair was turned into a wig for her to wear when she was working on her other job.[13]

This movie is based on a best-selling book by Jodi Picoult, but the movie and the book have almost opposite endings. You may want to check them both out to see which one you like best.

You can get a copy of this film, released June 26, 2009, wherever movies are sold and rented.

all the energy in the family is redirected toward your sib who is fighting for his or her life.

Even if you understand why you are getting less attention, it doesn't make the situation any easier. Welcome to the club. It is a big club, and there are many ways to get support from other teens who are experiencing the same thing.

There is no right way to feel. Talk to your family and friends. Write it all out in a journal. If you are worried that you will get cancer too, the chances are you won't. Most cancers don't run in families, but it is a good idea to talk to your family doctor for more information.

Megan

When I learned my sister had cancer all I knew about cancer was that you could die. I was pretty scared. I didn't know what to do. When she got cancer again, I was angry—angry at life in general.

The first time I had to be packed from home to home because my parents were at the hospital all the time. I don't want to say I felt abandoned because I knew my parents had to do that, but I felt alone. I would think that Amber was getting all the attention, and then a few minutes later I would remember that she was really sick. I knew I needed to grow up and work on helping her to get better.

The second time, I was old enough to stay alone, so I had to cook for myself and find a ride to school. I grew up pretty fast. Usually someone would take me to the hospital after school, but some nights I would just go to someone's house or my house. On the weekends, I would spend the night with her.

When I was at school, I would be thinking about Amber, and everyone else would be thinking about who they had a crush on. Watching someone go through cancer helps you understand that life is precious, and you can't take anything for granted.[14]

* * *

When you deal with your parents, remember they are under stress and may not always do or say what feels best for you. When your parents do have time for you, try to make the most of it. Make sure they know how much it means to you and keep talking. Don't feel guilty about wanting to have your needs met. Your parents love you too.

If you feel like your parents can't meet your needs, reach out to others who can help you. Consider grandparents, aunts, uncles, family friends, neighbors, friends of your parents, teachers, school nurses, coaches, and guidance counselors. They can help you too.

You can help your brother or sister in his or her fight against cancer. Just being together can mean a lot, watching movies together and hanging out. Help your brother or sister stay in touch with friends. Turn a snack into a picnic. Get matching hats for you both if he or she is dealing with baldness.

You will need to take care of your own needs too. Spend time with friends and stay involved in what you love. Get enough sleep. Switch to caffeine-free drinks in the evening that won't keep you awake. Try to make healthy choices. You know what they are.

Addie

I was fifteen to eighteen while my brother [Peter] was fighting cancer. I felt horribly scared. I felt like I had to be with him every possible moment. As time went on, I felt afraid to move on with my life because he wasn't able to.

This was the time when he should have been starting college. Then I got to that age, and he was still at home and in the hospital a lot. I was very hesitant to do what I was supposed to be doing at the time. It seemed very important to me to be there with him.

It's hard to think about what I was going through because I was so focused on what he was going through. My problems just didn't seem important to me or anyone else. I guess we never really sat down and talked about what the rest of the siblings were going through emotionally, but that would have been a good thing to do.

Now I'm thinking about taking the nursing certification. I have become interested in that through Peter. Through caring for him when he had cancer and watching the amazing nurses that he had in the hospital.[15]

* * *

Stay connected to your friends, and remember that they may not know what to say to you about the cancer in your family. You may have to take the first step. You can ask them if they have any questions. Or if you don't feel like talking about it, you can ask them if you can talk about it later.

There are some great websites that can put you in touch with other teens who have sibs with cancer at the end of this chapter.

Megan

What Fighting Cancer with Your Sister Can Teach You

"Amber has leukemia." I didn't cry. I didn't even react. My parents started to explain what was going to happen next, but I wasn't listening.

Old people get cancer—not my sister.

We were in the Family Conference Room and my mom was pulling at my limp hand. I had heard her say we were going to Amber's room. I hesitated, but slowly stood up and trailed behind them. What am I going to say to her? Do I act like nothing's wrong, or do I hold her while she cries?

Walking down the halls, looking in the gloomy hospital rooms, I saw so many weary parents. Babies were hooked up to IVs. My hands began to feel clammy, and my legs were shaking. We stopped at Room 453. Amber was sitting on the bed, her soft brown curls falling around her olive-colored face. She was smiling. She didn't look sad at all. She looked beautiful, laughing at some stupid joke my dad was making about doctors.

After a few minutes, or hours, the doctor we would all grow to know so well walked into the room. He starting explaining the treatment in what sounded like a foreign language. A bone marrow test? Methotrexate? What is this stuff? I knew my family didn't understand either, but they nodded anyway. My parents were holding hands, and I felt so alone.

In the weeks that followed the diagnosis, I became the forgotten child. My dad had to work a lot, and my mom didn't want Amber to be alone. I never complained. I knew what my job was. Just keep my grades up, keep a smile on my face. I didn't realize it would be so hard.

I watched cancer destroy my sister. Her hair fell out. Her eyes became tired. Her breathing was labored. They put a port in so they could administer drugs and take blood without having to poke her arms all the time.

When I looked at her, I didn't see my sister. I knew she was still Amber on the inside, but she was completely different on the outside. Cancer had taken its toll on Amber and on the rest of my family too.

My parents were weary all the time, and they looked aged. They looked at me, but they didn't see me. On the nights I spent at the hospital, I sometimes watched my sister sleep. Her face was scrunched up in pain, and I could feel it too.

Three years after the diagnosis, my sister's cancer was in remission, and things were finally getting back to normal. One day shortly after school started, I was home sick, and my mom and Amber were at the hospital for a routine checkup.

There was a knock at the door. It was the associate pastor from our church, and I thought I must be in trouble. I opened the door and felt the Alabama heat rush over me. I stared at him, waiting to hear what I was in trouble for.

"Your mom and Amber are at the hospital."

"Yeah, thanks. I know that." I even gave him a smart-alecky look.

"Amber's spinal tap results came back. She's relapsed."

My heat dropped into my stomach like lead. I was crying, and I hated showing weakness, and I hated people feeling sorry for me. Allen hugged me. I hated him. I hated my mom. Why couldn't she have told me? I made a mental note to yell at her when I saw her.

"Your mom wants me to bring you to the hospital, so get what you need."

I walked to my room and shut the door. As I leaned against it, I wiped the tears from my eyes and pulled myself together. I remembered what my mom had said three years ago. "You have to be strong for her, Megan." And I would be.

I climbed into Allen's car and settled myself into a position that showed I didn't want to be bothered. We didn't speak the whole thirty minutes to Children's Hospital. I was still mad at him, although I didn't know why.

As we walked into the hospital, I could hear the recording of the lady that welcomes you. I'd heard that lady a thousand times before. She welcomes you and tells you where to go when you leave the hospital. Then she says it all again in Spanish. I had it memorized in English and Spanish.

Allen was following me now. He knew nothing about the hospital. We walked past the nurses' station. They all knew me, but in that moment, I wished they didn't. My sister was sitting on the exam table. Everything about this moment seemed exactly like three years ago, but now we knew what to expect.

"Hey kiddo," she said and hugged me. I could feel the tenseness in her body despite the carefree look she showed on her face. I eyed mom and decided not to yell at her.

This time, as the doctor read the chemo schedule, there were no questions in my mind. This time the chemo was more intense. Amber got sick faster and stayed sick most of the time. She was in the hospital for weeks that sometimes dragged into months. We spent Thanksgiving in the hospital and got to go home just in time for Christmas. Life was crazy.

I was now old enough to stay home alone and was by myself most of the time. I spent the nights at my house alone and got myself up for school and found a ride each day. My parents couldn't help this. I knew it. There I was, acting like an adult, and fending for myself. My friends never knew how good they had it.

The worst thing that happened to them during the week was that some boy didn't like them. Big deal! I had to figure out what I was going to cook for myself that night. I would listen to them complain. Sometimes they caught themselves in mid complaint.

"Sorry, I know you don't want to hear this," they would say. I would just shake my head, reassuring them that all was well, and they would return to their "crisis."

One day in English class the intercom beeped as our principal came on for an announcement. "Sorry for the interruption, teachers. Many of you know Amber Luchterhand. We just got a call saying that she has taken a turn for the worst. I know we will all keep Amber and her family in our prayers during this time."

The room was silent. I looked up at my classmates. They were all turned to look at me, and I saw the sympathy in their eyes that I hated. I don't know why people feel sorry for me. Our teacher called everyone's attention back to Robert Frost. I stared down at my book pretending to read. Right then a single tear fell onto The Road Not Taken. I had seen my sister last night. I was with her. She was fine. They don't even know what they are talking about.

But she wasn't fine. Amber ended up in the Intensive Care Unit because of a blood clot in her port. The first few days I didn't want to see her like that, but soon I was ready to be there for her, like I always will be.

Now, when I look back on the five years since Amber's first diagnosis, I can hardly believe how far we've come. It may sound weird to most people, and maybe even a little demented, but I wouldn't trade the experiences cancer has given me and my family for anything, and I know Amber feels the same.

Cancer is a teacher. I've learned more from it than I could from any school. I had to switch from a kid to a mature thinker, and I missed out on a lot of childhood. I'm o.k. with that now because this has made me a better person, and I've made closer friends than I could have made before. Now that my sister is healthy, a full year being cancer free, I can honestly say that the toughest and most tragic times in a person's life can bring them memories that will last a life time.[16]

* * *

NOTES

1. Amber Luchterhand, interview with author, October 21, 2008.
2. Dr. Carol Diamond, associate professor, School of Medicine and Public Health, University of Wisconsin–Madison, interview with author, August 4, 2008.
3. Amanda Nicholls, interview with author, December 13, 2009.
4. Peter Greenwood, interview with author, August 20, 2008.
5. National Cancer Institute, "Bone Marrow Transplantation and Peripheral Blood Stem Cell Transplantation," reviewed September 24, 2010, www.cancer.gov/cancertopics/factsheet/ Therapy/bone-marrow-transplant (accessed December 7, 2010).
6. Juliette Walker, interview with author, September 7, 2008.
7. A. Luchterhand, interview.
8. Chelsea Prochnow, interview with author, August 27, 2008.
9. Patrick Dempsey, "Patrick's Story," Patrick Dempsey Center for Cancer Hope & Healing, www.dempseycenter.org/content/4078/ Patricks_Story/ (accessed March 20, 2010).
10. Patrick Dempsey Center for Cancer Hope & Healing, www .dempseycenter.org/ (accessed March 20, 2010).
11. Chase Prochnow, interview with author, December 10, 2009.
12. The Internet Movie Database, "*My Sister's Keeper* (2009)," www.imdb.com/title/tt1078588/ (accessed March 20, 2010).
13. Internet Movie Database, "Trivia for *My Sister's Keeper* (2009)," www.imdb.com/title/tt1078588/trivia (accessed March 20, 2010).
14. Megan Luchterhand, interview with author, December 7, 2009.
15. Addie Greenwood, interview with author, December 17, 2009.
16. Megan Luchterhand, excerpts from personal memoir.

RESOURCES

Gilda's Club is a place for people with cancer and their families to come together and build social and emotional support. They offer support groups for teens and social activities. You can call or check online to find if there is a Gilda's Club near you.

1-800-445-3248
www.gildasclub.org

Kids Konnected offers friendship, education, and support for kids who have a parent with cancer or who have lost a parent to cancer. They have programs focused on teens. Someone is there to talk to twenty-four hours a day, if you have questions or if you just need someone to listen.

1-800-899-2866
www.kidskonnected.org

Cancer Really Sucks! is a website designed for teenagers by teenagers with loved ones who are facing cancer. It has a special "How to Deal" section and also a place where teens can post stories about their situations, ask other teens questions, and speak with professionals through live chat and much more.

www.cancerreallysucks.org/index.php?page=Home

SuperSibs! is a great website. Click on the sib spot and then check out what they have for sixteen- to nineteen-year-olds. You can find teen teleconferences, podcasts, and video clips by sibs and for sibs.

www.supersibs.org

Your Shout is an online community for teens with a brother or sister with a disability or chronic illness. You can add them as a group through Facebook.

www.liquidsalt.com.au/yourshout/

The National Cancer Institute has published a cool guide for teens called *When Your Brother or Sister Has Cancer*. This is something you can download and print out.

www.cancer.gov/cancertopics/When-Your-Sibling-Has-Cancer/PDF

The National Cancer Institute has also published a booklet called *When Your Parent Has Cancer*, which you can download and print out.

www.cancer.gov/cancertopics/When-Your-Parent-Has-Cancer
-Guide-for-Teens/PDF

4 **Friends for Life**

Friends are really, really important. But when you get cancer, friendship for you and for your friends can become complicated. They may not know what to say. They may be frightened for you. No one likes to think about illness and dying, but you may be reminding people of those things just by having cancer. Some of your friends may not be able to handle it, but your true friends will.

As soon as you are diagnosed, everything is different for you and your friends. Try to understand how your friends feel, and let them know how you feel. As many teens before you have found out, there are ways to successfully deal with friendship during cancer. You can come out of this with social skills you never thought you had in you.

Cancer makes you realize what is good in life, and what's bad, and who your true friends are.

—Amanda Nicholls[1]

Seth

My friends supported me very well during the whole process. I learned about life. I learned that you find out who your friends are. When my friends found out I had cancer, they supported me. One of my best friends, he tried to make me feel comfortable. We never discussed the cancer. We just did our regular activities we would normally do, but maybe a bit more quietly because during treatment I was tired and more fatigued than normal.

When I was in high school, I wasn't a guy who would stand up and say things. I was the shy, quiet one. But after I was done with cancer, it opened me up. I had a whole new set of eyes

Seth on his way to class. *Courtesy of Seth Paulson.*

about how I saw life. That is part of the cancer experience. We only get one life, and we have to make good use of it because we are only on this planet once.[2]

Amber

I didn't want to say, "I have cancer," to my friends at first. I felt that if I said it out loud, that would make it too true. My mom brought one of my friends to the hospital. She didn't say a word to me. She just crawled in bed with me, and we both cried.

Then I called my friend who had moved out of state. It was really hard because I actually had to say it. I started having a normal conversation with her, and then I said, "I have something bad to say."

And she said, "What?"

I said, "I have leukemia."

And she was like, "Oh, my gosh!" She told me that the night before she had watched a movie about someone with cancer, and she told me, "Something in my heart told me something was wrong, and that I should call you, but I was afraid to."

She would write me really long letters. I would call her from the hospital and talk for four hours at a time.

It's really good sometimes to have friends going through the same thing you are going through. And it's good to have friends who aren't. My friends who weren't going through the same thing encouraged me because I saw a

Damian and Libby, fellow cancer survivors. *Courtesy of Elizabeth Falck and Damian Buchman.*

normal life, and what normal life could be, and I wanted to fight for that.[3]

*   *   *

"At first, their friends initially will be all over the place. You have friends everywhere," says Dr. Puccetti, "but then as things go on, especially if it's a chronic type of cancer or with recurrences, then they are not seeing their friends. You see less and less friends. It's really sad. Everyone in the beginning is right there, but then I think for those friends, they see their friend in trouble and they don't know what to say. Adults don't even always know what to say when we are faced with these things."[4]

Whether you are at the hospital or back in your school building, you can take charge of how cancer will affect your relationships. Some friendships may fade but don't assume the worst.

Some people may not mention your cancer and act as if they don't know what you are going through. They may not know what to say and may be worried about making things worse by saying the wrong thing. If you feel like you are being left out of activities you used to share with friends, it may be because they aren't sure what you are able to do and don't want to make you feel bad. They may also feel guilty about having fun when you are not, and the easiest way to deal with that is to avoid you.

It can go the other way too. You may want to avoid your old friends. Cancer can make you extremely close to your family at a time when your friends are all moving away from their families emotionally and bonding with their peers. You can feel pulled out of your social network and be dealing with doctors while your friends are graduating from high school and moving on to college.

Another barrier you may feel to old friends is a drastic difference in priorities. Battling for your life is not what teens are usually focusing on, but if you have cancer, you are confronting issues that many adults don't even want to face. Being wise beyond your years can have its upside, but is doesn't make it any easier to jump in when your friends are talking about fashion or football.

Amber

Not Today! An Excerpt from Amber's Memoir

When I don't feel good, I don't like to be around people. I don't feel like talking. I don't feel like listening. I just feel like existing.

And I DON'T want to talk about it. You might see me with a blank stare on my face or even frowning, but don't be shocked. I've felt like crap for a few years, and I think it's finally catching up with me.

When I'm in this mood, which I'm labeling "reflective," I don't want to be bothered. I don't want you to tell me things are going to work out fine. I also don't want you to call me with some dumb story about what happened to you today. I don't care. Not today. Not while I'm feeling like this.[5]

Libby

There are a lot of reasons why cancer makes friendship hard. The main thing is physical differences. Most kids who go through cancer look different in some way or maybe they can't run or even walk.

The bigger difference is that once you've been through something like cancer, you have been pretty close to death. Pretty much every one with cancer has had some moment when they didn't think they were going to make it. When your friends at school are talking about their bad hair day, and maybe you don't have any hair at all—that makes it difficult to relate to them.

I was thirteen when I got cancer the first time, and I was pretty much out of school the whole year. I was being treated two hours away from home, and it was hard for my friends to deal with it. Going back to school was difficult. I was really quiet. I had one really great friend who stuck with me the whole time. In high school, she would push me to classes in my wheelchair. But for most people, it was too time-consuming to deal with me.

A lot of people say that when you go through something difficult, it makes you appreciate your life more, and I think that's true. I feel like I'm a lot more comfortable with people who are older than me than with people my own age.[6]

Peter

Cancer gives you a filter. You can tell the people who are good people. You go through something like that, and you need people to have your back, and you find out the people who can. I don't take it personally if they can't, but they won't be my best friends.

There are other people who just didn't know how to deal with it. They didn't know how to respond. Coping with this stuff when you are young and have cancer, you are forced into it—you have no choice. But your friends may have a hard time dealing with the realities of how cruel life can be, and how

Peter writing a song. *Courtesy of Peter Greenwood.*

it's not fair what happens to some people. If you are sixteen to eighteen, you may not be ready to realize that. It's not something you can fault them for, but if they can't be there for you—it makes it hard.

Cancer probably affects how I make new friends. I'm more the type of person now who has some really good friends, rather than a lot of people I just know. I mean a lot of my friends now, they are not necessarily way older, but they are not as young as I am.[7]

*   *   *

Your best friends will be there for you, but with that realm of pretty good friends, you may have to work a little harder. Take the lead. Call your friends and invite them over. You can set the pace and pick activities you feel up to taking on. This will cue your friends about the kind of things you can and want to do while you are in treatment.

Juliette

I think it was a shock for my friends. A lot of my close friends were good about it. They were visiting me in the hospital and keeping me updated. They would come to my house because I couldn't go anywhere, and they just sat with me.[8]

Chelsea

When my mom had cancer, my friends could be a source of frustration. Sometimes I wanted so badly for them to understand, and sometimes it was just, "You don't understand—just let me be." Some of my friends experienced it with me, and they have a new perspective on life too.[9]

* * *

Your friends probably don't know much about cancer. You are getting a crash course, but how much did you know before your diagnosis? Others probably won't feel comfortable bringing up the topic. They don't want to stress you. Let them know whether or not it is okay to ask you how you are feeling, and make sure they know the answer to that question can change at any time. It's up to you to tell them in a way that it is no big deal. Be matter of fact about your treatment, and share any details if you want, or simply say that you are getting treatment and are hopeful. You are in charge of what information you share.

Jon Michael

I feel like if I know someone well enough, then I tell them I had cancer. I don't say it on the first handshake of meeting

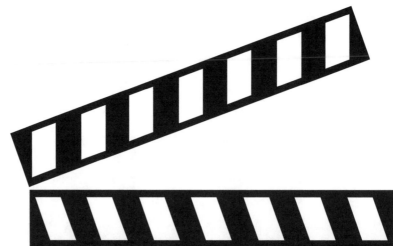

GOOD FILM: *Crazy Sexy Cancer*

Just weeks after being diagnosed with a rare and incurable form of cancer, thirty-one-year-old actress Kris Carr turned the camera on herself as she embarked on the fight of her life. The result is this moving and funny inspirational documentary. In need of experimental treatment, Carr travels the country seeking experts on alternative medicine and, along the way, meets other cancer-stricken women driven to survive.

This is a real, live story about an actual woman. She tells her own story, and she doesn't pull any punches. Kris has written a book by the same title, and both of them are crazy, sexy, irreverent, and uplifting. This is about a person with a strong will and driving curiosity following her own life or death journey.

Her film looks at her own experiences and also those of other people going through cancer treatment, mixing interviews and candid moments in a way that is never dull.

someone. I'm not embarrassed, but I just don't think it's the first thing I want to throw out about me. All my close friends know. I bring it up over time. It was a big part of my life, and I feel it made me a stronger person.[10]

Amanda

I look to my friends. I can go to them and talk to them anytime. If I really need someone to talk to, they will be there for me and listen when my mom can't listen or doesn't want to listen.[11]

Justin with award.
Courtesy of Justin Thomas.

Justin

Initially most people were shocked. Most of them knew me and never thought this could happen to me. "He is so healthy!" I was captain of both my football and wrestling teams.

My teammates were there for me. They dedicated the whole season to me, and my number was painted on the football field. At Senior Night I was honored to lead the team for warm-ups.[12]

Kenzie

I have great friends who came and visited me in the hospital and at home. Some people I thought were my friends, but I never heard a word from them that year. I guess if I were in their place, I wouldn't know what to say either. But at the time I wanted to know why they wouldn't talk to me. I understand better now.[13]

* * *

Cancer changes a lot of things in your life, and it will change your friendships too. Some friendships will become much deeper. Many people say that cancer teaches them about what is really important, and that knowledge can make friendships stronger.

Because you have cancer, you will meet other teens who also have cancer—people you would never have met in "normal" life. Some of these people will become best friends for life.

A good way to find other teens who are sharing your experience is through support groups and camps for people with cancer. There is a chapter in this book about the powerful effects of attending camp. Most of these camps are free or very low cost, and there is certainly one that is tailored to you. Check it out as soon as you can.

NOTES

1. Amanda Nicholls, interview with author, December 13, 2009.
2. Seth Paulson, interview with author, August 26, 2008.
3. Amber Luchterhand, interview with author, October 21, 2008.
4. Dr. Diane M. Puccetti, associate professor, School of Medicine and Public Health, University of Wisconsin–Madison, interview with author, August 5, 2008.
5. Amber Luchterhand, memoir, February 19, 2007.
6. Libby Falck, interview with author, December 14, 2009.
7. Peter Greenwood, interview with author, December 2, 2009.

8. Juliette Walker, interview with author, September 7, 2008.

9. Chelsea Prochnow, interview with author, August 27, 2008.

10. Jon Michael Gabrielson, interview with author, December 7, 2009.

11. Nicholls, interview.

12. Justin Thomas, interview with author, December 15, 2009.

13. Kenzie Derr, interview with author, December 21, 2009.

14. Answers.com, "Deborah Ann Kent," www.answers.com/topic/deborah-ann-kent (accessed March 20, 2010).

RESOURCES

2bMe is a website created as part of Look Good . . . Feel Better for Teens, a program of the American Cancer Society. It has a section called "Social Circles" that has good advice on how to cope when you are feeling self-conscious, tired, or just different.

www.2bme.org/2bMe.html

CancerCare has many services for young adults at its website. It offers support groups where you can connect with other cancer survivors your age. You can also connect with an oncology social worker in person or over the phone.

www.cancercare.org/get_help/special_progs/young_adults.php

Teens Living with Cancer is a website that can connect you with other teens who are dealing with cancer.

www.teenslivingwithcancer.org/

Group Loop is an online support group where teens talk to teens about their health, their home life, school, and friends. This is an amazing way to connect.

www.grouploop.org/#

Planet Cancer was founded by young adults between the ages of eighteen and forty who are surviving cancer. The website is designed to help young adults with cancer network with and empower each other. There are many ways to connect here.

www.planetcancer.org/html/welcome.php

5 Mirror, Mirror on the Wall

From the moment you are told you have cancer, you may feel differently about yourself and you may see yourself differently. Some of the changes are real, such as scars or having a part of your body removed. Some of those changes are just temporary, such as hair loss or changes in your skin or your weight.

Even if these changes are not permanent, they can still hurt you right here and now. It's natural to feel upset if your body changes, and it is an extra challenge to deal with these changes while you are suddenly looking at life and death in a very immediate way. Don't be surprised if you find yourself feeling frustration, fear, and fury, or even simply deep sadness. These feelings are normal. But it's not all bad.

There are other feelings that many people who have faced cancer often share. You may be amazed at how your body can stand up to punishing treatment. You may find yourself becoming more aware of how fragile life really is and treasuring the kind of moments you used to not even notice. You may realize that you have a lot to feel grateful for in a way you never did before your diagnosis.

I was worried about what everyone would think of me without hair and without a foot. I realize now I should have looked at the big picture.

—Kenzie Derr[1]

Amber

It's kind of gross. I didn't take a shower for a long time in the hospital. They just gave me sponge baths. My hair was in a pony tail. As soon as I got home, I wanted to wash my hair. When I did, it all came out at once.

69

SAFE SUN

The sun can feel really good on our skin, and the popularity of tanned skin is what keeps tanning salons in business, but if you are undergoing chemotherapy, you have to be especially careful about how much sun you get.

Certain chemotherapy drugs make the sun much more dangerous for you than others. You will burn while the person next to you will not.[2] And if you have been exposed to radiation treatments, you are more likely to get skin cancer from the sun.

Whether you are a cancer survivor or not, the sun is something you need to be careful about. More than 1 million people are diagnosed with non-melanoma skin cancer each year and sixty thousand get melanoma skin cancer, the most serious kind. But most of these skin cancers can be prevented by staying out of the sun and out the tanning parlors.

In general, too much sun increases your chances of getting skin cancer, and if you get sunburned when you are under twenty, that sunburn is even more likely to give you skin cancer.

Using sunscreen is important, but don't let it make you overconfident. Some research suggests that people usually don't apply enough sunscreen and don't reapply it when they should, but because they are wearing some sunscreen, they feel safe to increase their time in the sun, so they actually burn themselves worse. So don't forget your sunscreen, and slather it on.

A word about tanning salons: they can be dangerous. And like cosmetics, tanning facilities are not regulated. The World Health Organization thinks tanning equipment is so dangerous that it recommends the time that teens can spend on the tanning bed should be restricted. If you want to take care of yourself, consider skipping the tanning bed.[3]

Tips for Safe Sun

- Use a broad-spectrum (protects against UVA and UVB rays) sunscreen with a SPF (sun protection factor) of 15 or more. A SPF of 15 will block out 93 percent of burning sunrays.
- Put on sunscreen fifteen to twenty minutes before exposure to the sun.
- Use a thick layer and reapply it every two hours, especially if you are swimming or sweating.
- Stay out of the sun as much as you can between 10 a.m. and 4 p.m.
- Wear sunglasses to protect your eyes from exposure to UV light.
- Find and wear a hat you like with at least a four-inch-wide brim.[4]

I kind of laughed, which is not the normal reaction, but it was a panicky laugh.

I did get upset at the way people stare. When you are bald, they know you have cancer just by looking at you. It feels like you have to explain yourself to everyone. You don't have any privacy. If you go anywhere, people stare at you. It's not that they are trying to be rude. It's natural to stare.

Actually the second time, I knew I was going to lose my hair, so I cut it short because I thought it would be easier that way. When it started to fall out we just shaved it. My friends shaved it from the back of my head, and we made it into a fun thing instead of something sad.

My friends were always like, "We'll shave our heads." But I said, "No. I don't want you to do that."

I would wear a bandana instead of a hat because hats didn't fit me right. So my friends would wear bandanas with me.

My senior year is when I relapsed, and I wanted to have hair for prom and graduation. So we ended up buying a wig that I really liked. That is the only time I wore it. My hair is really curly, and I have to spend a lot of time on it.

Honestly, it was easier being bald!

I also went through a lot of weight fluctuations. When I first got sick, I got really skinny. I didn't feel really skinny, but when I looked in the mirror it would be, "Wow! I'm skin and bones."

They put me on steroids, and that made me gain a lot of weight. My cheeks were big and puffy and swollen. It was strange. That wasn't fun.

I don't know if you are ever really happy with yourself, but now I'm really happy to be healthy.[5]

*　*　*

It's not always possible to keep remembering the big picture when you are looking in the mirror, but there are things you can do to help yourself through this time.

Remember that knowledge is power and learn as much as you can about what to expect. Having a plan in place will make it a lot easier to see your hair start to come out.

Juliette

It was really hard to lose my hair. I had really long hair before. When I was diagnosed, I got it cut to chin length. It's hard to have it fall out. You want to keep it for as long as you can.

Juliette in her favorite hat. *Courtesy of Juliette Walker.*

Having it fall out at random times is a reminder all the time of the chemo and the pressure that is being put on your body. Yeah, it was hard to lose my hair, but once it was out, it wasn't that bad.

I got to wear lots of cute hats. It was kind of funny because I had a pass to wear hats in the hallway at school. Hats aren't really allowed in my school, so whenever I would walk down the hallway the teachers would say, "Take your hat off." I would say, "Actually I have a pass to wear this because of chemo."

It was kind of irritating, because I felt that people don't understand sometimes. But they learned eventually that I had a pass.[6]

*　*　*

Even if you try to prepare yourself, be prepared to take a while to get used to the changes you are seeing. And remember that if they are shocking to you, your friends and loved ones feel the same way. They may not know how to react. If you can bring a sense of humor to your situation, you will make it easier for yourself and let the people around you relax and feel comfortable with you. On the bright side, things like broken nails are never going to bother you again.

If you are having trouble finding the bright side, reach out to your parents, school counselor, or nurse. They can connect you with someone whose job it is to help people through these kinds of hard times.

Seth

I lost all my hair. I remember it was my second semester of classes at college. It started in my English class. I just lifted my hand to

LOCKS OF LOVE

Locks of Love provides hairpieces from donated hair to people under age twenty-one who have lost their hair to illness. These hairpieces would cost between $3,500 and $6,000, but people receive them for free or on a sliding scale, based on financial need.

They are different from synthetic hairpieces because they form a vacuum seal on the head and do not require tape or glue. People can swim and shower with them on. When someone is accepted into the program, a molding kit is sent to make a plaster cast mold of the person's head. This is what creates the special seal.

This is a great way to help someone. It takes six to ten donated ponytails to make one hairpiece, so the need is great. You will find Locks of Love contact information in the resources section at the end of the chapter.

Here are some of the donation guidelines:

- Hair must be in a ponytail or braid *before* it is cut.
- Ten inches of hair measured tip to tip is the minimum needed. Curly hair may be pulled straight to measure it.
- Layered hair is okay if the longest layer is at least ten inches.
- Hair that is colored or permed is okay but hair that is bleached (including highlights) is *not* okay.
- Hair is needed from men and women, young and old, in all colors (blond, brunette, auburn, etc.) and from all races.
- About 80 percent of all donations come from young people who wish to help other young people.[7]

scratch my head, and I pulled a big chunk of my hair out. I knew I had to go through it, but I thought, "This really sucks!"

Sometimes I would cover my baldness because I guess I was a little self conscious of what people might think of me. I'd never been bald before. But toward the end, I didn't really wear anything because my hair was starting to come back, and it looked like a buzz cut.

When it did start to fall out, my hair came out in big clumps, and you could see little bald spots, so I just went to Cost Cutters and got my whole head shaven off. I quickened the process. Some people don't do that, but I think when I had my head

⊚ ⊚

DELTA GOODREM BEATS LYMPHOMA

Australian singer-songwriter and actress Delta Goodrem's life seemed like a dream come true when she was signed by Sony at age fifteen. But at age eighteen, Delta was diagnosed with Hodgkin's lymphoma. She was quoted on Contactmusic.com as saying,

> I was completely shocked when they told me. I was so upset, so totally upset. But deep down, despite the shock, I wasn't actually surprised. I'd found this lump and pushed any negative thoughts to the back of my mind but my imagination was racing. The hardest thing was trying to take it all in.
>
> Then within a few hours of being told by the doctors, my illness was on the news. I felt totally crazy. I sort of shut down emotionally because I didn't know how to deal with it. Luckily I was surrounded by my family who love me, good friends and amazing doctors who helped me understand exactly what was happening.[8]

Lymphoma is a form of cancer that attacks the body's immune system. Like many cancer patients, Delta underwent chemotherapy and radiation therapy, and lost her hair for a time. She remembers, "It's weird to see pictures of that time. In some ways the fact that I was so sick was so out there, and yet I kept it really private. No one saw me on the days I was really sick. I was 18 when I was diagnosed, and I had a number one album and single in the country. And in the UK, I was number two. It was such a bipolar year."[9]

As soon as Delta's cancer was in remission, she began work on her second album and established the Delta Goodrem Leukemia and Lymphoma Research Trust Fund, and she now spends part of her time promoting cancer charities. A percentage from the sale of each ticket from her Visualize tour was donated to the trust fund she established. On tour she thanked her fans for their outpouring of support during her fight with cancer. Much of her album *Mistaken Identity* was inspired by her battle, especially "Extraordinary Day." She also helped launch Teen Info on Cancer, a United Kingdom website that supports teen cancer patients. She has also been the face of Alternative Hair, a fund-raiser of the hairstylist industry in Britain.[10]

shaved, it looked better. Some people look good, you know, bald. I may have looked a little funky—not the greatest—but I thought I looked good myself. I was probably just boosting my self-image.

When it grew back, I left my hair short like it is now. Every now and then I'll get a buzz cut, but if it's a nice day, I like the wind blowing through my hair.

My friends ignored my baldness. I think they supported me. I don't think it was a big deal to them. We all knew it was going to happen eventually. Every now and then they would crack a few jokes to try and make me laugh about it. That's how you find out who your good friends are.

After treatment, I started reading articles on Yahoo! about what to eat after having cancer. Basically it said eat healthier with lots of fruit and juice. Less soda, more juice and water. Try and get in shape. Things like that. It's a good thing. Working out is a great way to relieve stress. I feel good now.

I've seen people with pink doo-rags or bandanas to cover their baldness up. I know what they are going through. It's kind of a cool style for them. I respect the style they are trying to achieve. Every now and then I see people who are bald. I don't bring it up. Everyone is different, and I don't know how they would react.[11]

*   *   *

BAD HAIR DAY

You have chemotherapy and radiation therapy to fight the fast-growing cells that are your cancer. That same therapy will harm the cells that make hair because they are growing fast too. That means that hair on your head or anywhere on your body may fall out. Your hair may start to fall out two to three weeks after therapy begins.

You may be able to slow down the hair loss process by washing your hair with a mild shampoo and patting it very gently to dry. Forget about hair dryers and hair products like gels or clips. Some people decide to cut their hair very short so they don't feel such a loss when it starts to fall out.

Justin

My hair fell out. My hair was completely gone from every inch of my body. Eyelashes—everything. I just had eyebrows.

I had just got out of the hospital, and I was going to see *Harry Potter 3*. I put some grease in my hand to rub in my hair. I rubbed my head, and something wasn't feeling right. I pulled my hand down, and it was full of hair. I just kept pulling it out and playing with it.

I knew it was falling out, but I actually laughed. Laughing was my way to deal with not crying about it.

My hair has always been curly and wavy but now it is even more curly and wavy. Some people call me Fuzzy Wuzzy. Hey, I can take a joke.[12]

*   *   *

Most likely, your hair will grow back in two to three months after your treatment. It might grow back curlier or straighter or even a different color than it was before. It may gradually go back to the way it was before treatment. It's a wait-and-see game.

In the meantime, protect your head from the sun and from the cold in the usual ways that bald people must. Use sunscreen. Wear a hat or scarf. You may even find it more comfortable to sleep in a soft scarf.

Losing your hair may be hard for you, especially at first. Talking about your feelings with friends and family can help. You may want to join a cancer support group, where you can share your feelings with other people in the same place as you, and also share ideas about how to cope.[13]

Work with your stylist. He or she may have experience with helping people style through cancer treatment. Your hospital may even have an in-house image center.

Debi Machotka is the Positive Image Center cosmetologist at American Family Children's Hospital in Madison, Wisconsin. She has helped many teens find their best look during cancer treatment.

"There is no right or wrong time to make decisions about your hair," she says.

You will know when the time is right. One girl was so traumatized that she just sat in here and cried for a whole hour. I saw her a few months later, and she was completely bald and okay with it. She was focusing on makeup and drawing more attention to her eyes and lips.

Initially, I thought girls would want to have a wig, but
once they get them, they are often not wearing them. They
are warm and uncomfortable. Your scalp is so sensitive when
you are going through treatment that a three-quarter wig with
a headband may be less confining. It fits more snugly to the
head. Another great option is a doo-rag with hair stitched on.
Motorcyclists like to use this. It gives good coverage and is very
light weight.[14]

CAN MAKEUP INCREASE YOUR CHANCE OF GETTING BREAST CANCER?

How can that strawberry-sundae blush that gives you such
a healthy glow be bad for you? This is a case where beauty
is more than skin deep. You may be layering lead onto your
lips, making your lashes longer with a coating of mercury,
and slathering your skin with a lotion that is loaded with
carcinogens.[15]

Why should teens be especially concerned about this?
Because you are growing really fast in your teen years, and
chemicals that alter hormonal development can hit you really
hard. According to the Environmental Working Group, teens
may be particularly sensitive to exposures to chemicals like
the sixteen substances examined in their study. Your body is
working hard to transform you from a child into an adult. It
is making changes in your reproductive system, your immune
system, and your brain's structure and function that will be part
of who you are for the rest of your life. This is not a time to be
adding more toxic chemicals into the mix.

That raspberry lip gloss may cost more than you want to
pay. Some chemicals common in cosmetics that were found in
this test have been linked to cancer in laboratory studies. Some
of them have been linked to falling levels of fertility, especially
for American women under age twenty-five. Some of the
dangers include increasing rates of breast and prostate cancer,
diabetes, and obesity.

Everyone wants to grow up as quickly as possible, but over
the last four decades, the age at which girls hit puberty has been
getting earlier. If you enter puberty at an early age, one side

effect is that you are at a greater risk of getting adult diseases, including breast cancer. Early-maturing girls are also more prone to problems such as depression and eating disorders, among others.

Doesn't the government protect us from dangerous, harmful things like this? Not in this case. The U.S. Food and Drug Administration (FDA) does not have safety standards to protect teens from potentially harmful ingredients in makeup or other body care products. The FDA does not test personal care products before they are sold, and it doesn't have the power to recall a product that turns out to be harmful.

As a teen, you are taking your first steps toward independence and you are developing your own style. Since the government can't protect you, you are going to have to develop a style that protects yourself. It's important to know that makeup companies can say whatever they want about their products. No one is watching them. You have to keep your eyes open when you choose your eye shadow or liner.

It sounds like a lot to keep track of, but knowledge is power. Learning to be on the lookout for these chemicals can keep you safer now and in the future.

Here are a few things to keep in mind when you are shopping:

- ◎ **Use fewer, simpler products.**
- ◎ **Don't trust claims like "dermatologist tested," "natural," or "organic." Read the ingredients label for yourself.**
- ◎ **Take warning labels seriously. They are talking about hazardous chemicals.**
- ◎ **Before buying a product, look it up at the Environmental Working Group's consmeticsdatabase.com.**

If this seems like the kind of issue you want to get involved with, check out the Campaign for Safe Cosmetics. You'll find the website in the resource section at the end of this chapter.

Brittany

I've been in the newspaper, so most of the world has seen me bald. When I first got diagnosed and I had a rare blood type, my

COSMETIC CHEMICALS TO BE ON THE LOOKOUT FOR

Phthalates (pronounced THA-lates) can interfere with your hormones. This is a common ingredient in nail polish and is also used to moisturize and help chemicals absorb into the skin. It may not be listed in the ingredients, but it could still be in there. Studies of people exposed to phthalates show they can have increased risk of reproductive system problems and give birth to babies with birth defects. Phthalates are considered hazardous waste and are regulated as pollutants in air and water, but they can also be used in many everyday products. No, this does not make sense. It does mean that you have to be on your guard. You can reduce your contact with this hazardous substance by choosing products that don't list "fragrance" as an ingredient.

Triclosan is used to kill bacteria on the skin and other surfaces. But though it may seem like a healthy choice to use it, you are actually putting yourself at risk. Triclosan is often found in antibacterial liquid hand soaps as well as and in toothpastes, deodorants, face and body washes, and acne treatments. This chemical can accumulate in fat and builds up in your body over time. It can react with chlorine in tap water to create chloroform, which is suspected of causing cancer.

Musks are artificial chemicals used in fragrance mixtures added to many products. They are used in perfumes, soaps, air fresheners, and cleaning products. Musks can be absorbed through the skin or inhaled. If you use them regularly, they will build up in your body. Musks can interfere with the ability of structures in cell walls to keep toxic substances from entering your cells. One way to reduce your exposure is to switch to fragrance-free cosmetics and body care products.

Parabens are used to keep germs and mold from growing in cosmetics and body care products in order to increase their shelf life. They may be included in your moisturizer, skin cleanser, shampoo, conditioner, sunscreen, deodorant, shaving gel, and toothpaste as well as your makeup. They can irritate your skin, or worse, they can disrupt your hormone system.[16]

mom called the newspapers and asked people to donate for me. I was dying. She did blood drives and bone marrow drives. I got the blood I needed.

I lost my hair, my eyebrows, and my eyelashes. I don't think that really fazed me. My thought was that if you don't like me, that's your problem.

It did make me more aware of how sick I was. Now that I have my hair again, I don't want to cut it. It's my pride, and it's gotten curlier.[17]

* * *

SKIN PROBLEMS

Your skin may become very sensitive during your treatment, and it is going to need tender, loving care. Always wash your face in warm water with a mild soap that rinses off easily. Be sure to use a light sunscreen, and make sure your doctor approves of the ingredients.

If you are having radiation therapy, be extra careful to make sure your doctor approves everything you put on your skin (including makeup). On the areas of skin that have been treated with radiation, just rinse them with water. Pat—don't rub—that skin to dry it and do not scratch or shave it.

Amanda

My hair was brownish-blond, and it was past my shoulders. When it started falling out, I cut it to my shoulders. My doctor said to go ahead and shave it, but I didn't want to. In a way, I thought I was winning over cancer as long as I still had my hair.

When it first fell out, this girl at school said I was faking and stuff. I had people saying, "Oh my gosh! Why are you wearing that?" because I would wear a bandana.

I wasn't going to wear a wig. A wig is not me. It wasn't easy, but I wanted to get over it. I had a job. I worked at a clothing store in the mall, but they stopped using me when I lost my hair. They said they wanted their employees to have hair. It was discrimination. I thought I'd be the bigger person and ignore them, so I quit. I've got a better job now.

My hair is growing back now. It's a couple of inches long.

My other issue is that the cancer makes spots. It is over much of my skin. It's on my arms and my back and my stomach and legs. If I wear a bathing suit, people can see it. As long as I wear a shirt with sleeves on them and long pants, people can't see it. They don't hurt, they are just like a pigment in the skin. They really don't bother me. It's a part of my life now, but I try not to let people know I have cancer. I try to hide it. I don't want them to judge me by it or feel sorry for me.[18]

* * *

SCARRED BY THE PAST

The heat also reminded me of something else I have yet to face . . . short sleeves. I don't think I've mentioned it (mostly because I'm ashamed), but when I had the blood clot and was in the ICU, I gained a lot of weight. Within a matter of hours, I was so swollen that I was almost unrecognizable.

Well, because of this weight gain, I have stretch marks—BAD ones. The most embarrassing ones are on my arms. I've tried different lotions and junk, but I know they'll never completely go away. It makes me so angry. I've worn long sleeves ever since.

I can't look at myself in the mirror without being disgusted. I know it's not my fault . . . maybe it would be easier to accept if it HAD been my fault, if I had eaten myself into obesity and stretch marks. But I didn't. And now I'm forever scarred. I can't even wear a simple t-shirt. The marks come down to my elbows. I'm so ashamed . . . worried about what other people who don't know me will think. And if I can't stand to look at myself, I wouldn't dare subject the world to this.

In June I have to wear a bridesmaids dress. Spaghetti strapped. I shudder to think of it. But it's for Briana. I'll suck it up, try and make do with make up and wear the dress. I'm so tired of hiding.

I can't wear long sleeves forever. Even in the 75 or 80 degree weather it's miserable. I remember when I used to be self-conscious about my scar on my chest and my port. I used to try to find clothes that would cover them up. Wow, I wish that was my only clothing worry now.

Life shouldn't be this hard at 18. I should be able to wear the cute clothes that I want to. I should feel comfortable dating guys. But the truth is I don't want to date. And most of it has to do with my body. How can I let someone love me if I don't love myself?

Anyways, enough about that. It's just depressing. I know you all will have something to say about it . . . that I'm beautiful or whatever. You have to understand. I love MYSELF. I HATE my body.

And it's not even that I hate my body. I just hate how it's scarred by my past . . . a past that I wish I could just leave behind me.—Excerpt from a cancer survivor's journal

If you are having chemotherapy, you need to stay away from hormone creams and anything containing hydrocortisone. You should also keep out of the sun, but if you can't dodge the sunshine, stay slathered in sunscreen. Chemo can make your skin feel dry, so be ready to use a doctor-approved moisturizer whenever you feel itchy. Make sure you aren't using anything like astringents or strong acne treatments—anything that has alcohol is going to be drying.

Remember that cancer treatments can compromise your immune system, so be extra careful about hygiene. You have to be a bit like a doctor prepping for surgery and wash your hands very well before you put anything on your face. Treat your jars carefully to keep them from becoming colonies of germs by using cotton balls, swabs, or disposable applicators. Above all (and this may be the hardest), *no sharing* with friends. Germs that they don't even notice could get a free pass on your vulnerable skin. Don't give them that chance.[19]

YOUR LOOKS AND YOUR OUTLOOK

Cancer changes you. Appearance, self-perception, and self-esteem are linked. It's easy to look into the mirror and feel down or defeated. But look deeper. You are still in there, stronger and better than ever.

Peter

Now that I'm a cancer survivor, being an amputee has hit me. The cancer treatment is over, but I'm going to be an amputee for the rest of my life. Where am I at as a disabled person? I established my identity as an able-bodied person for almost twenty years. I don't know.

I feel like recently I have gotten to the point where I can let myself say I have a disability. If I'm wearing pants, people don't even notice. Sometimes when I have on shorts, they don't even notice. This thing is amazing. There is a computer chip in it. There is metallic liquid in the joint, and the computer will sense the terrain and how fast I'm walking and reprogram itself to control a magnetic field that makes the liquid harder or more fluid.

I've noticed when I'm stepping into the throw of a baseball it tightens up, and then when I start walking, it loosens up again. It's like anybody else walks. You don't have to think about your walking. To get back to that point, it's amazing just to be able to walk.

There are things that are difficult but basically, I feel totally fortunate. I played soccer and basketball, and when I'm out on my hand cycle, I get a lot of exercise now, but still, riding by a basketball court or soccer field is one of the hardest things I have to do on a regular basis because there is part of me that just wants to get out there and go.

Even now.

It's funny because my brain is still having the instincts it used to have. I'll go to catch a ball, and part of my body shoots out there, but the rest of me can't get there fast enough.[20]

* * *

Take charge of your appearance and learn what you can do if you want to modify it. 2bMe is a website created as part of Look Good . . . Feel Better for Teens program of the American Cancer Society. Its four sections are "About Face," "Head Way," "Health Esteem," and "Social Circles." This is the place to get some help with your skin and hair problems and to find tips on how to keep as fit as possible. You'll find the website in the resources at the end of this chapter.

2bMe also offers free two-hour workshops for teens of both sexes around the country at eighteen hospitals that treat teens with cancer. The workshop includes lectures and hands-on sessions. Each teen leaves with a free kit of personal care items and a take-home guide. Check the website to see if there is a hospital offering this workshop near you.

How we look is important to us all. Skin problems, weight fluctuations, and hair loss make public what's going on with us. But even hidden scars and the need to be extra careful about germs or getting overtired can make you feel different from others and self-conscious. If what you are going through is temporary, hang on and ride it out.

Try to find a group in your area or online where you can talk with other teens about how they deal with these issues. Be prepared for people to be startled by the outward signs that you are fighting cancer and be ready with all the answers you feel comfortable giving. You get to decide what to share and what is private.

You may look different. You may feel different. But you know that stranger in the mirror. The same things that have made you who you are will still be there during cancer treatment and beyond.

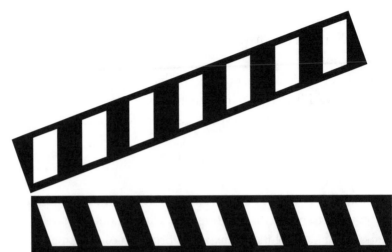

GOOD FILM: *The Breast Cancer Diaries*

Television news reporter and young mother Anne Murray Paige chronicles her nine-month battle with breast cancer in this poignant, insightful, and humorous documentary directed by news correspondent Linda Pattillo. Sharing her thoughts in a video diary, Anne gives a raw view into the life-altering journey taken by one in seven women worldwide, and challenges an emphasis on physical appearance as she rules out breast reconstruction.

Anne says, "Hearing all this awful information about your self is mind-boggling. Snapping into 'reporter mode' was the way I dealt with it without emotionally imploding at the same time."

Linda started filming Anne three days after her diagnosis, and she has caught the highs and lows and everything in between. Between them, they have created a window into the world of a young woman and mother with breast cancer.

"Our hope," says Anne, "is to give hope to the people who surround those diagnosed with breast cancer: to offer them insights on how to help, how to be a friend, and what it's like to have cancer at a young age, with so much to live for. I'd like it if this documentary brings hope for the future of those of us whose lives are forever changed thanks to cancer."

You can get a DVD of this film at the website.[21]

NOTES

1. Kenzie Derr, interview with author, December 21, 2009.

2. DermNet NZ, "Skin Toxicity of Chemotherapy Drugs," www .dermnet.org.nz/reactions/chemotherapy-toxicity.html (accessed March 22, 2010).

3. National Cancer Institute, "Sun Protection," *Cancer Trends Progress Report—2009/2010 Update*, last reviewed January 7, 2008, progressreport.cancer.gov/doc_detail.asp?pid=1&did=2007&chid=7 1&coid=711&mid (accessed March 22, 2010).

4. National Children's Cancer Society, *The Mountain You Have Climbed: A Young Adult's Guide to Childhood Cancer Survivorship: Beyond the Cure*, p. 13, www.nationalchildrenscancersociety.org/ NetCommunity/Document.Doc?id=51 (accessed March 22, 2010).

5. Amber Luchterhand, interview with author, December 4, 2009.

6. Juliette Walker, interview with author, September 7, 2008.

7. Locks of Love, "Donate Hair," www.nexxus.com/locks-of-love (accessed January 3, 2010).

8. Contactmusic.com, "Delta Goodrem's Cancer Moment Shock," December 11, 2003, www.contactmusic.com/new/xmlfeed .nsf/story/delta-goodrem.s-cancer-moment-shock (accessed March 22, 2010).

9. Jean Kittson, "Delta Goodrem," *OK!* 1 (October 2004): 37.

10. Anlin00, "Delta Goodrem—Cancer," YouTube, www .youtube.com/watch?v=0roTLfS3i5w (accessed March 22, 2010).

11. Seth Paulson, interview with author, August 26, 2008.

12. Justin Thomas, interview with author, December 15, 2009.

13. National Cancer Institute, "Hair Loss (Alopecia)," posted November 24, 2008, www.cancer.gov/cancertopics/chemo-side-effects/hairloss (accessed January 3, 2010).

14. Debi Machotka, cosmetologist, Positive Image Center, American Family Children's Hospital, Madison, Wisconsin, interview with author, August 6, 2009.

15. Sarah Moran, "Look Past Surface for Beauty Products," *StarTribune.com*, November 1, 2009, www.startribune.com/lifestyle/ style/67769112.html?page=1&c=y (accessed March 22, 2010).

16. Environmental Working Group, "Teen Girls' Body Burden of Hormone-Altering Cosmetic Chemicals," September 24, 2008, www .ewg.org/book/export/html/26953 (accessed March 22, 2010).

17. Brittany Hill, interview with author, December 21, 2009.

18. Amanda Nicholls, interview with author, December 13, 2009.

19. Look Good . . . Feel Better, "Makeup Step-by-Step," www .lookgoodfeelbetter.org/women/make_over_steps/skin_care .htm#requirement (accessed January 3, 2010).

20. Peter Greenwood, interview with author, December 2, 2009.

21. The Breast Cancer Diaries, www.thebreastcancerdiaries.com/ (accessed March 22, 2010).

RESOURCES

Locks of Love
234 Southern Blvd.
West Palm Beach, Florida 33405

Locks of Love provides hairpieces to young cancer patients. Maybe you need help from Locks of Love, or maybe you are thinking about donating your hair.

www.nexxus.com/locks-of-love

2bMe is a website created as part of Look Good . . . Feel Better for Teens program of the American Cancer Society. Its four sections are "About Face," "Head Way," "Health Esteem," and "Social Circles." They will help you with your skin, which may be acting weird, and your hair, which may be falling out. They also have a section on how to ramp up your fitness, and give your body, skin, and hair a boost at a time when they really need it.

www.2bme.org/2bMe.html

Teens Living with Cancer is a website where teens talk about body issues such as losing their hair, dealing with treatment side effects, and just about everything else.

www.teenslivingwithcancer.org/i-can-deal-with-it/body-issues/

Coping with Changes to Your Body is a good web page supported by Cancer.Net.

www.cancer.net/patient/Coping/Age-Specific+Information/
Cancer+in+Teens/Cancer+and+Your+Body/Coping+With+
Changes+to+Your+Body

The Campaign for Safe Cosmetics is a good website to check out if you would like to work toward safer cosmetics.

www.safecosmetics.org/

6 Camp and Other Comforts

Summer camp has always been a place to learn a few survival skills and build up your strength in the great outdoors. For those with cancer, survival skills mean more than just how to make a fire or pitch a tent. There are camps out there that can provide medical support you while you are undergoing chemotherapy, and there are also programs to support you while you figure out what to do with the rest of your life as a cancer survivor.

This is the one place where you are not different from everyone else.

—Libby Falck[1]

JUST JUMP IN

Though some teens may resist the idea of a camp for cancer patients, they usually find it is one of their most powerful aids to readjustment. It's like jumping into a mountain spring. The water looks cold, and it is cold, but once you take the plunge, you never look back.

"It's always kind of hard to get kids to go the first time, but I've never hear of anyone who didn't love camp after they had been there," says Libby Falck, who was diagnosed with bone cancer in her right leg at age five.

> Going to cancer camp was the last thing I wanted to do. It was all about making friends in my school. I felt like going would set me apart from my friends and make me even more different. So I didn't go until two years after I finished treatment. At fifteen, I finally went. For the first time I didn't have to worry about being different.

After you go, you realize that this is the one place where you are not different from everyone else. Everyone else has gone through the same thing and it's just the most incredible feeling. I had never known what that was like.[2]

After attending Camp Silver Lining in Colorado at age fifteen, Libby went to Camp One Step at a Time when she was seventeen. She is still going back in her early twenties, but now she goes as a counselor.

BECOMING A CAMP COUNSELOR

Many camps were originally established for younger campers. These camps have adapted to the growing number of older teen and young adults who have cancer by creating counselor-in-training programs.

A good example is the EXCEL program at Camp One Step. The EXCEL program is for teens ages seventeen to twenty-nine. Many teen counselors have already spent summers at Camp One Step and are ready to challenge themselves. In this program, you take charge of preparing, organizing, and leading an all-camp activity, and you come away with the skills that can help you overcome life's challenges.

"I don't think it was a big deal to become a counselor," says Libby Falck. "With Camp One Step, a lot of people start going when they are young and turn into counselors when they are nineteen. When I started at One Step, I was already in the age group considered a counselor-in-training.

"You are still a camper, and you start working with the younger kids, so you are not in charge of any of your friends. I love being a counselor. There is extra responsibility, but it is fun to be working with the younger kids and essentially play all day. Because of camp, I have the job I have now."[3]

Libby now works at the National Ability Center through AmeriCorps, where she leads a program on adaptive skiing for skiers with physical disabilities in Utah. The Ability Center offers a broad range of sports programs and outdoor activities for individuals with both physical and developmental disabilities.

Libby

In some cases where somebody has gone through the same cancer I had, or they are going to have a similar operation or treatment, I have been able to tell them what to expect. My cancers were relatively common for teenagers, so I have several friends who have had salvage surgery and the same treatments and chemos. We can relate about that kind of thing. But when you go to a camp like this, the majority of kids are already survivors. Even kids in treatment have usually been in treatment for many years. Giving advice isn't something we tend to do a lot of.

Libby on skis. *Courtesy of Elizabeth Falck.*

We all understand. Sometimes we share stories, but the focus of the camp is to be able to forget about all that stuff for once. We want to totally let it go and ignore it.

It's really a great community for kids with cancer. It's a great way to feel normal, no matter what your disability is. You feel that way at camp, and you can carry that confidence and knowledge that you are not alone with you wherever you go.

Camping totally changed my life and what I wanted to do. It made me feel like it was okay to work from the experience of being a cancer camper and start volunteering for other organizations. Before camp that was something I tried to stay away from.

After camp, I got involved with the American Cancer Society and founded my own organization, Teens Tackling Cancer. We were a small group of kids in Wisconsin and Illinois, and we helped each other with our treatments and did a few events. The group brought us together outside of camp and gave us another opportunity to socialize.[4]

*   *   *

CAMPS FOR EVERY NEED

There are many camps for kids who have cancer in their lives so you can find just the experience that fits your needs. One of

FIRST DESCENTS

If you come to First Descents, you will prove to yourself and to everyone that cancer is not stronger than you are. This is a camp that is all about having fun, getting outside, and pushing your limits.

It all started with Brad Ludden, who has been a professional kayak athlete since he was sixteen. "At first I was working with younger teens," says Brad. "Then we started to see that late teens and early twenties are a group that is really underserved, and we switched to working with people in that group. We have found that our participants feel disconnected at diagnosis and don't know where to turn."

First Descents is there to put you outdoors in a legitimate challenge. "Teaching people skills and letting them apply those skills can restore a lot of confidence in [their bodies]," says Brad. "It allows people to take back the self-control that was lost with their diagnosis. Also, a really strong bond forms between participants. Whether you are on a rock wall or kayaking through rapids, there is a level of trust created in the group. At the end of the week, campers have regained a lot of things that the cancer took, and they have created bonds with others that may have been missing in their lives before the program."

The First Descents program is the new kid on the cancer camp block. It started in 2001. In 2009 the camp served 250 people. By 2015, Brad says, "we hope to have 1,000 campers a year, but we will still limit each individual program to 15 for safety reasons and to make sure everyone gets to connect with the people in their group."

The program is branching out beyond kayaking. "We are partnering with some of the really competent and reputable outdoor adventure companies to customize the experience for our programs based on what people want and their ability," says Brad. "For example, we take rock climbing instructors, and we train them to be First Descent counselors. It's a great mix. As an outdoor guide, you are already passionate about your work. Learning to share that experience with someone who is using it as a form of therapy—this makes a big impact on the guides as well as the campers."

"People mostly find us by word of mouth," Brad says. "We are connected to 35 major medical centers. Our referrals come from social workers or fellow survivors. We have tried to make it simple. Just go to the website. [You'll find it in the resources section at the end of this chapter.] You can download an application and submit it online."[5]

the newer camps out there is First Descents. This program is for people who want to reclaim their sense of adventure. When it began, First Descents focused on kayaking and taught campers to shoot rapids and even dive down waterfalls.

"I love it," says Peter Greenwood, who has lost a leg to cancer. "Whitewater is something else. Brad, the founder, is one of the best whitewater kayakers in the world. I have had ex-Olympians teaching me at camp. You have great support.

CAMP SMILE-A-MILE

Camp Smile-a-Mile on Lake Martin in Alabama, or as campers call it, Camp Sam, provides year-round opportunities for cancer patients and former cancer patients. This camp is only for Alabama residents, but it is typical of the kind of camps offered throughout the United States and Canada.

Like many cancer camps, it started as a destination for children, and has grown as the teen and young adult cancer population has grown. "We noticed that there was a definite need for survivors of childhood cancer," says Jennifer Queen, Camp Sam's program director. "In 1993 when I first started in oncology camping, the survival rate for kids was 50 percent. Now it can be 80 percent or greater, and these kids have new challenges as survivors. Camp Sam offers Teen Camp for teens, ages thirteen to sixteen, and Junior/Senior Weekend Camp for high school juniors and seniors."

Several years ago, Camp Sam started offering a Young Adult Retreat for childhood cancer survivors in the nineteen to thirties age group. "Once you are considered a survivor," says Jennifer, "you move forward with your life, and especially as you get out of high school, there are a lot of decisions to make." The retreat focuses on long-term survivorship issues like insurance, singleness, time management, independent living, and jobs. "You can get stuck in a rut," Jennifer says. "You may still think you are a cancer patient. You need to see yourself as a survivor and move forward. That's what this camp provides."

"Also," she continues, "the majority of our young adult group went to this camp when they were younger. They know each other very well. They can talk to each other bluntly and hold each other accountable, which is fantastic. They are a great support to each other."

"And," she concludes, "whenever you come to camp, it's a chance to be a kid again."[6]

They start you out on the lake and show you how to wet exit a kayak. You progress to higher and higher rapids. Depending on the group, you may be doing class 3 rapids." (According to the rapids rating chart, class 3 means "waves numerous, high, irregular; dangerous rocks; boiling eddies; rapids with passages clear though narrow, requiring expertise in maneuvering; scouting usually needed. Requires good operator and boat."[7])

"Having that common experience with a bunch of other survivors is really good," says Peter. "You get that communal feeling right away working on something that is hard to do. It's a major adrenalin rush. I went from never doing it before to last summer going off some waterfalls. It's a great experience. I've seen it really transform people, and it happens fast."[8]

If you don't want to, you don't have to shoot rapids. Every camp sets up an environment that lets campers find what they need.

Amber

Camp is great. I am so glad I went. I had a lot of fun, but more than that, I had people to talk to who had a better chance of understanding me than most people do. At the candle lighting ceremony, I found myself mourning more than just the loss of fellow campers. I mourned the things that cancer has held us back from doing. I mourned the way life used to be. But camp is a place for happiness, and I found that there too.

It's helpful to talk with friends who had cancer and to see what they were going through. I got to meet people with all different kinds of cancer. I got to see all the different things that cancer can do to people, but at camp we don't tend to talk about cancer. It's a place where we can all be the same. You are not the kid with cancer there. People don't have questions or stare.[9]

* * *

Amber started attending Camp Smile-a-Mile when she was fifteen. Now that she is twenty, she has been to its weekend retreat aimed at the needs of young adult survivors. "They bring in people who can talk to us about nutrition for cancer survivors and people who can talk about the effects of chemotherapy that we have to deal with. It's really a weekend workshop with a chance to see the people you went to camp with when you were younger," she says.

"It helps to share experiences and to learn how to take care of your body because cancer survivors have higher risks for pretty much everything."[10]

CAMPS FOR SIBLINGS

Because cancer affects everyone in the family, many camps offer special programs for kids who have brothers or sisters with cancer. Siblings sometimes feel forgotten and alone when their

CAMP STAR

A song by Justin Thomas, inspired at camp

It's a new day—I cleaned my room.
Quick somebody grab me a broom!
We are so tired of being hurt
Cause we really want to be first.
I woke up a moment ago.
Head outside, let's start the road
To be a camp star
We'll go far.

Justin belting out "Camp Star." *Courtesy of Justin Thomas.*

Sometime soon they're on the way.
It's a good thing that we mopped today.
We brushed our teeth and made our beds
Doing what they expect.
We went as far as to clean the air
That's how much you know we care
To be a camp star.
And we'll go far
Tell me what it takes to be a camp star.

This is camp Smile-a-Mile.
Didn't want to leave, so I stayed a while.
I've met so many friends,
I'll do anything to come back again.
They are the reason why I sing,
And that's why I'm going to be
A camp star.
We'll go far
To be a camp star
Tell me what it takes to be a camp star.
I got to know now
So I can be.
Show me the way to be a camp star.
Just take me, so I can be a camp star.
Yeah, yeah, be a camp star.
We'll go far.

Justin explains how he came up with this song:

One day I was in the cabin relaxing during bunk time. This guy was playing his guitar, and I started singing, "I want to be a bunk star." I started making words up, and we wrote it down and performed it. People loved it. It was instantly a hit. It swept the campground, and people were singing it all over.

When I attended the memorial for people who had died that year, that was a new idea to me. I never knew anyone who had died from cancer. I wanted to make the song more memorable, so I changed it to camp star and added a serious verse.

Two years later people are still singing that song.[11]

SUPPORT GROUPS

Camps can be a great source of support, but what do you do for support when you are not at camp? There are many groups out there who know what you are going through and are ready to connect.

Planet Cancer is a community of young adults with cancer, who are at that age "where no one knows whether to give you a lollipop or have a serious talk about your fiber intake. It's a place to share insights, explore our fears, laugh, or even give the finger to cancer with others who just plain get it. We don't deny the dark side of illness and death here. But we also firmly believe that laughter and light can turn up in the strangest places."[12]

At this website, you will find support groups you can join listed by state. You can also join web groups divided into categories like Bone Marrow Transplant Survivors, the Cancer Knot (about weddings and cancer), People Who Couldn't Have Gotten through This without Their Pets, Students, and Young Lung Cancer. (Contact information for these groups can be found in the resources section.)

sick brother or sister is receiving most of the attention due to his or her treatments. Sibling camp is a chance to do something that is just about them, get some well-needed attention and have fun in the process.

Check the program list of a camp's website for sibling activities. For example, Camp One Step at a Time, listed in the resources section, has a program just for sibs, and so does Camp Smile-a-Mile.

BUT WHAT DOES IT COST?

Most camps for young people with cancer do not charge campers. If they do, it is usually a fraction of the actual cost of the camp, and those fees may be dropped if your family cannot handle them. The organizers of these camps understand the financial blow that a major illness deals to any family.

Before you write off the idea of camping as too expensive, read up on the camp you are interested in. If it is not actually free of charge, the camp staff should be able to help you get to camp.

NOTES

1. Libby Falck, interview with author, September 4, 2008.
2. Falck, interview.
3. Falck, interview.
4. Falck, interview.
5. Brad Ludden, interview with author, December 7, 2009. See also First Descents website, www.firstdescents.org/ (accessed January 3, 2010).

6. Jennifer Queen, program director, Camp Smile-a-Mile, Birmingham, Alabama, interview with author, December 10, 2009.

7. Wikipedia, "International Scale of River Difficulty," en.wikipedia.org/wiki/International_Scale_of_River_Difficulty (accessed January 3, 2010).

8. Peter Greenwood, interview with author, August 20, 2008.

9. Amber Luchterhand, interview with author, October 21, 2008.

10. Luchterhand, interview.

11. Justin Thomas, interview with author, December 15, 2009.

12. Planet Cancer, "Welcome," www.planetcancer.org/welcometopc/ (accessed January 4, 2010).

RESOURCES

Association of Hole in the Wall Camps
265 Church St., Suite 503
New Haven, Connecticut 06510

Though Hole in the Wall Camps are for ages seven through sixteen with varying medical conditions, you will find many fellow cancer survivors there. If you are older, many camps offer counselor-in-training programs, where you can train to become a counselor.

www.holeinthewallcamps.org

Camp Māk-a-Dream
P.O. Box 1450
Missoula, Montana 59806

This program offers teen camp and siblings' camp as well as camps for young adult cancer patients and young adult cancer survivors. Patients come from all over the United States and Canada and are assured their medical needs will be taken care of. The Young Adult Survivors Conference is a six-day educational program that builds bridges of support among young adult cancer survivors who can help each other navigate the health care system, relationships, employment, and more.

www.campdream.org

Camp One Step at a Time
213 W. Institute Place
Suite 511
Chicago, Illinois 60610
312-924-4220

This program serves young cancer survivors up to age nineteen
who live in Illinois, Indiana, Wisconsin, Michigan, and Iowa. It
never turns a child away for financial reasons. It offers camping
programs in Wisconsin and organizes whitewater rafting and
outdoor adventure in North Carolina. There are classes for
siblings of cancer patients as well.

www.onestepcamp.org/

Camp Ronald McDonald for Good Times
5640 Apple Canyon Road
P.O. Box 35
Mountain Center, California 92561

This sixty-acre camp in the mountains offers camps for patients
and siblings ages sixteen to eighteen all year long. Kids come
here from across the United States and the world.

www.campronaldmcdonald.org/

Camp Smile-a-Mile
P.O. Box 550155
Birmingham, Alabama 35255
205-323-8427

This camp is specifically aimed at cancer survivors who live
in Alabama. It offers a family camp for therapy patients up
to eighteen and their immediate families, as well as programs
for young people who have completed treatment. It also has
special programs for high school juniors and seniors, and a
Young Adult Retreat for nineteen- to thirty-year-olds aimed
at teaching them about long-term survivorship issues such as
insurance, singleness, time management, independent living,
and healthy lifestyles.

www.campsam.org/index.asp

Children's Oncology Camping Association International

This is a great site to find a camp near you. This web page displays a map of the United States. You can click on any state to see what camps are offered there and then follow up to find out about their programs and age limits.

www.cocai.org/cocai.org/membercamps/index.html

First Descents
P.O. Box 2193
Vail, Colorado 81658
970-927-2444

This camp will challenge everything you thought you knew about yourself. First Descents describes its program this way: "First Descents is not just giving young adults with cancer their self-confidence back, we're also connecting a largely disconnected population. First Descents helps shatter the illusion that cancer makes people fragile."

www.firstdescents.org/

Planet Cancer Re-Orientations
314 E. Highland Mall Blvd.
Suite 306
Austin, Texas 78752

Planet Cancer is aimed at young adults. It sponsors weekend retreats for people diagnosed with cancer, ages eighteen to twenty-five. Spend the weekend at a re-orientation and find a new sense of normal networking to share hard-won wisdom, soaking in info from expert guest speakers on topics from insurance to handling stress and participating in recreational outlets such as rock climbing and games.

www.planetcancer.org/

7

Cancer and Your Classroom

Everyone is different. You have to tune into where you are now. School may not be that easy. You may have short- or long-term learning challenges from your treatments. At the same time, you may also find that you have motivation you didn't have before. Cancer makes you more mature, and you may have more sense of purpose than you did before.

Communication is the key. Keep talking with both your teachers and your fellow students.

There is no education like adversity.

—Benjamin Disraeli[1]

KEEP TALKING WITH YOUR TEACHERS

Your teachers need to know what challenges you are facing and how they can help you learn. Ask your parents to help let your teachers, school nurse, and guidance counselor know what is going on with you. Check to see if your hospital has someone who works directly with schools.

Libby

I worked really hard in school to get all my requirements done. It was pretty hard as a freshman and sophomore with so many doctors' appointments, but it paid off. I had a tutor who was supposed to teach me, but he had been a math teacher and he only cared about teaching math. That was pretty much the only thing I learned that year. Still, I graduated a year early and had AP credits.[2]

Juliette

I started cancer treatment in March of my junior year. I didn't go to school at all for a while. I wasn't able to do anything. The chemo I was on was really intense. I was completely exhausted, and I couldn't be around crowds of people because I couldn't have any germs.

My junior year I had to drastically cut my schedule down so I could work on making up stuff and continue with the classes I really needed. I worked over the summer so I could graduate at the regular time.

> **☑ Your hospital may have someone who can help you coordinate with your school. Be sure to ask.**

Some of my teachers were really good about it, but I don't think some of my teachers understood why I hadn't been doing my school work. I was going through a lot while I wasn't there. I wasn't just skipping. I obviously wanted to do as much as I could.

It was especially hard because my high school hasn't had many people who have had to deal with cancer in the past ten years, so they really didn't know what to do with me.[3]

* * *

> **☑ You may be absent a lot and find it hard to keep up with school work. Your doctor can help you estimate how much time that your treatment may take.**

If you need to be out of school or miss a lot of classes because of your treatment, try to keep connected with your school. As a teen, school is your most important job, but getting healthy is your biggest challenge at the moment. The balance between healing and homework is something each person has to work out for themselves.

Catching up can be hard. Work with your teachers to stay on top of your work as much as possible even during treatment. Keep them in the loop about where you are medically.

Ask for help. Perhaps you can get a friend to take notes for you when you have to miss class. Make sure your teacher knows your friend is taking your notes, and the teacher may be able to help him or her keep you up to date. Your teachers may be able to share the notes they use to teach or record the classes for you. Some teachers are even willing to e-mail you assignments that you have missed.

Justin

Everyone in my school was shocked when I got cancer the summer after my junior year. Most of them knew me because I was captain of the football and wrestling teams. I would walk around the school, and any teacher would speak to me. I was very close to my principal, and I was active in everything.

Everyone was worried when I missed the first two weeks my senior year. When they saw me, they said, "You've got a bald head. Did you go to jail or something?" People who didn't know me were talking about my head. I didn't want people to be talking bad about me. I felt like beating them up, but I had to restrain myself.

The ones who knew me supported me. My whole school and community supported me. They nominated me for the Brian Jordan's Athletic Scholarship for athletes who do well on the field and in school. It did help me out. I didn't have to pay anything for my first year of college. They also nominated me for Alabama Public Television Young Heroes of 2008.

Cancer was the end of my sports career, but I have a new goal now to succeed in theater. I worked hard my senior year. I ended up going back to coach, and I did two plays my senior year. That was my way of fighting—to say, "I am not going to give up." You have to push forward and find ways out of this situation.[5]

 GOOD READ: *Side Effects* **by Amy Goldman Koss**

This is a book about a young woman who fights cancer and lives. Izzy is a fifteen-year-old trying to live a normal life. When she should be coping with what shirt to wear, instead she is struggling with the side effects of chemotherapy to combat lymphoma. One reader says, "Izzy narrates with a very sarcastic view on her disease. Although there's nothing funny about cancer, Izzy keeps a smart, witty sense of humor even at the hardest of times."[4] *Side Effects* follows Izzy's crazy journey in her own voice and lets you feel like you are hearing it from your best friend.

As if it doesn't suck enough to have cancer, practically every time you pick up books or see movies where characters get sick, you know they'll be dead by the last scene. In reality, kids get all kinds of cancers, go through unspeakable torture and painful treatments, but walk away fine in the end. From the acclaimed author of *The Girls* and *Poison Ivy*, *Side Effects* is about the pain, fear, and unlikely comedy of fifteen-year-old Izzy's journey, told in her own powerful and authentic voice. It is Izzy's story—screams and all.

Publisher: Roaring Brook Press
Publication Date: 2006
Pages: 143

> ☑️ **Ask friends to take notes for you, and make sure your teacher knows they are doing this so he or she can help them.**

(Justin continued as president of his high school's Interact club, which undertakes clean-up jobs in the community, and of GUMBO [Groups Understanding Multiple Blends of Students], and he served as a mentor to academically challenged students through the Big Brothers/Big Sisters program.)

Jon Michael majoring in creative writing. *Courtesy of Jon Michael Gabrielson.*

* * *

CANCER, STRESS, AND YOGA

Regular physical education (PE) classes may not be possible when you have cancer. Yoga may be a good alternative for several reasons. Yoga can provide a good work out that you can adjust to your needs and energy levels. Yoga can also help you cope with stress.

Battling cancer is one of the most stressful things you can do. On top of that, you have to contend with the side effects of your treatments. This means more stress. When doctors talk about stress, they mean the response of the body to physical, mental, or emotional pressure, which may cause unhealthy chemical changes in your body. Untreated stress may lead to even more mental and physical health problems.

Your body responds to stress by releasing stress hormones, such as adrenaline, that create the fight-or-flight syndrome. This would be handy if you were jumping out of the way of an oncoming train, but doesn't help you when the stresses are caused by cancer and its treatment. To heal as quickly as possible from cancer, it is important to try to control your stress levels.

Harvard University neuroscientist Sat Bir Khalsa recently did a study with high school students in Massachusetts to compare students who did twelve weeks of yoga with another group assigned to regular PE class. At the end of the program, students filled out questionnaires, and the students practicing yoga reported less anger and fatigue and more resilience than those who took regular PE class. Students who learned yoga said they found their yoga skill was a good tool to deal with stress.[6]

Studies have linked stress to how tumors grow and spread, but researchers don't yet really understand how this happens. Stress can affect your immune system, which may affect the growth of some tumors. No studies have shown that stress can cause cancer, but there are studies that connect your psychological state and cancer development.[7]

Many people feel that yoga is a good way to control stress, and research is now being done to see if yoga can help cancer patients in particular. The National Cancer Institute is working on a clinical trial to study the effects of yoga on fatigue and sleep in cancer patients who are undergoing chemotherapy.

They are also studying how yoga can affect mental health and stress levels.[8]

One study at the University of Texas found that cancer patients who practiced yoga were less tired and felt less sleepy in the daytime. The people in the study said they felt better when they practiced yoga.[9]

The National Cancer Institute says that stress-reduction programs tailored to the cancer setting may help cancer patients cope with the acute effects of treatment and improve quality of life after treatment, and that yoga may be particularly useful to reduce stress and speed recovery.[10]

Brittany

They had a school in my hospital. A nurse came to my room and asked me if I wanted to go to the school, and I looked at her like she was crazy, like, "I'm sick! I don't want to learn right now. I didn't want to worry about anything. I just wanted to get healthy and go back to my real school." But then I realized that she was trying to give me some kind of normalcy in my life.[11]

* * *

You may be able to negotiate a reduced homework load with individual teachers, or you may need to work with your guidance counselor to cut back on some classes.

You may look normal to the people around you, but you may have serious information processing issues to deal with. "Radiation to the brain and some chemotherapy techniques can cause problems with information processing. You can probably tell if you are feeling different about your memory or concentration now," says Dr. Diane M. Puccetti.[12] You are going to need to take charge of finding out what your learning issues are so that they don't submarine the rest of your schooling.

> ☑ **You may have to scale back on your class load and focus on core classes like math and English.**

GOOD FILM: *Healing Cancer from the Inside Out*

Filmmaker and researcher Mike Anderson questions the validity of conventional cancer treatments and offers a natural alternative for healing the body through nutrition and supplements in this comprehensive, two-part documentary. In this film Mike shares his ideas about how to assess the benefits and risks of any cancer therapy. Researchers, nutrition experts, and cancer survivors also offer inspiring testimony to natural healing.

Many people have tried to find alternative cancer treatments, and this is a controversial area. The treatments that Mike shows have not been tested scientifically like those that your doctor depends on. He is promoting the idea that the cure for cancer will not be found under a microscope but on your dinner plate.

What you eat can impact on your health, so this film might give you some ideas on what you can do to power your healing process.

You can find this film, released in 2008, wherever films are rented or sold.

Some cancer treatments can cause learning problems. You may be aware of them right away, or they may come up much later. Mathematics, spatial relationships, problem solving, attention span, reading and spelling, planning, organizing, and concentrating can all be affected. Problems with fine motor skill might even cause poor handwriting.[13]

You may find it harder to maintain alertness in general, especially if you are bored. When coming out of cancer, it's hard to maintain your enthusiasm and focus, and some things in school are not all that interesting. It's very easy to let your thoughts drift. Your brain may be working at a lower processing speed now, which means you can miss information and fall behind. You need to let your teachers and parents know right away if you feel this happening to you.[14]

Amber

My high school was really helpful. The counselors set up a homebound teacher for me who would help me with my school work. I liked her as a person, but I didn't like having her looking over my shoulder.

I'm kind of an independent worker. I could learn on my own. I would just do my homework by myself. It was challenging with the algebra, but I managed, and I came out with some pretty good grades.

I did end up having to get help from the teachers when I really needed it. I got to go to school about half my sophomore year and my whole junior year. It was good to be around people and learn in a classroom, but it was also an adjustment after you have taught yourself for a year and a half.

I missed my whole senior year except for the first month. But I still participated in a lot of things like the school play and musical *Anything Goes*. I got to play a character completely opposite from myself, and that was fun. I had a lead part in that. I was sick for most of the rehearsals. It was a miracle that I could perform all three shows. That's something I'm really proud of from that time. It took a lot of drive.

There are studies that show that chemo actually kills brain cells. It makes you—I don't want to say dumber, but it inhibits your ability to really think. I've noticed that. I used to be really, really smart, and I'm still pretty smart, but it takes me longer to figure things out now—especially math.

It's really hard to think things through sometimes. My head just goes kind of cloudy.

Cancer and moving right after high school really set me back. Since I was first diagnosed, I have felt behind, but don't feel that way now that I am back in school. Now that I'm actually doing something, I feel much better.

I started back to school in August at Blackhawk Technical College. I'm hoping to get into their nursing program, and I'm excited about it. I want to give back to the nursing field because of everything that I've been through.

Some of the nurses who treated me had been through the cancer thing, and it was cool to talk to them and hear their success stories. I've been around the medical field so much, that it comes pretty easy to me. Right now I'm taking anatomy and physiology, and I'm doing pretty well.

I'm comfortable at a technical college because I was worried about being older than the other students. I'm twenty-one, and there are a lot of people way older than me, so it's easy to get involved and not feel uncomfortable.[15]

Amanda

I'm on a special plan to work part of the school day. It excuses my absences from school, and it gives me more time to make up my work. Most of my teachers are sympathetic, but some are like, "You're an adult now, and you should be able to manage your time and stuff."

I used to be in band, but the band director didn't understand that because I have cancer, I can't be outside when it's freezing cold and raining. In band camp we don't get water breaks, and I need a certain amount of water. I passed out at band camp, and had to go to the hospital and have an IV.

Amanda, self-portrait. *Courtesy of Amanda J. Nicholls.*

I have a job to help pay for my insurance. I'm also saving money for college. I want to be a pediatric oncology nurse practitioner. I want to use my cancer as a way to teach people.

Make sure your teachers know that you are doing your best and that you appreciate their help.

A lot of people didn't know how to respond to my cancer. I've been in the school newspaper twice about it now. It's a day-to-day job, helping people learn about cancer.[16]

*   *   *

SMOKING—DON'T DO IT!

Today another two thousand people under eighteen years old in the United States became regular cigarette smokers. The good news is that number is down from three thousand a day in the 1990s. The bad news is that nearly seven hundred of those smokers will die early due to lung cancer or other tobacco-related diseases.[17] Or put another way, one-third of the 1 million teens who start smoking each year will die from their addiction. Picture three teens having a cigarette together. Survival statistics just drew a big X over one of them. Your treatment may have already put you at increased risk of lung problems, so you need to avoid smoking even more than most people.[18]

Being a cancer survivor does not mean being just like you were before. The treatments that stop cancer carry a double whammy. They also make you more prone to new cancers. You are also more likely to develop heart and lung disease—and when you add cigarettes to this picture, the risk increases.[19]

Smoking or using other tobacco products is risky for anyone, but it is even more risky for teens who are being treated for cancer. Studies are starting to show that smoking can make your cancer treatment less effective. It can reduce your tolerance for the treatment, increase the risk of complications, and make you more likely to get a secondary cancer. In the survival game, smoking stacks the deck against you.[20]

According to a 1994 U.S. Surgeon General report, health consequences of smoking start early. Young smokers without a history of cancer can expect to deal with respiratory symptoms and infections, reduced lung growth, increased coughing, and compromised physical activity. The complications for teens being treated for cancer are worse. Smoking may delay healing after surgery and slow down your return to your regular life.[21]

Perhaps smoking can seem like a way to reconnect with other teens after being forced into a world apart by your cancer and treatment. Research has shown that teens sometimes start smoking because they are experiencing stress. Stress is something that cancer survivors know all too well. Add that to the daily pressure about whether to start using cigarettes, alcohol, and other drugs. Talk about stress!

As a cancer survivor, you are and always will be at risk for health complications that can cut off your options. It is going to be your responsibility to take charge of your health, and that includes your decision about smoking.[22]

People who start smoking before the age of twenty-one have the hardest time quitting.[23] So if you haven't started smoking, you have managed to dodge a very big bullet.

If you have started smoking or are thinking about it, there are people out there who really want to help you. Your doctor or nurse is ready to bend over backwards if you reach out. They have seen the damage smoking can do, and they would rather help you now than deal with the grim consequences later.

KEEP TALKING TO YOUR FRIENDS

When you are ready to go back to school, keep your close friends close. Things may seem different—they probably are different—and your friends can help you move through unfamiliar situations.

Your friends may be unsure how to react and need some guidance from you. If you talk easily about your cancer, it will be easier for everyone else to know how to behave. Some teachers may even give you some time to talk to your class as a whole about your cancer. You will need to decide what you want to share and what you want to keep to yourself. You have the right to share only the information you are comfortable talking about.

> ☑ When your classmates first learn about your diagnosis, they will have different reactions, but many will want to help. You may want to talk to your class. Plan what to say ahead of time and decide how much information you want your classmates to know. If someone asks a question you don't want to answer, you can say, I'd rather not talk about that. You are entitled to as much privacy as you want. How much information you share with classmates is completely up to you.

Seth

School is going well. I have just three more classes, and I'll be done with a degree in graphic design.

I kept going to school while I was going through cancer treatment. I didn't want to let cancer affect me because I knew I was going to get through it, and I knew my cancer was a fast cancer, so I didn't let it stop me. I never looked down. I always looked up.

The beautiful thing about education was it took my mind off cancer. It caused me to focus on my studies. When I was in school, I didn't think about cancer.

At first I didn't want to tell anybody about my cancer. Maybe I felt embarrassed. But as I grew, I have learned not to run from my problems. You have to face them, and I have become more outspoken. I guess I was a little shy, but then I opened up and said, "Hey, I've got this. I don't want sympathy. I just want you to know." And people really cared.

My personality slowly grew out of this till now I am a fun-loving guy, always looking for someone to talk to and making new friends. I'm actually a really different person than the one who came out of high school.

In high school, you stick with one group, but in college, I'm making friends with people older than me and younger than me. I know forty-year-olds. And not only different age but ethnicity—the whole thing. College is great for networking.

I'm trying to find my niche in graphic design. I'm good at logos, magazine spreads, stationary. Anything, really. That's what I like about graphic design. You can express yourself.[24]

* * *

EDWARD KENNEDY JR. HELPED CHANGE THE ODDS

Edward (Ted), son of U.S. Senator Edward Kennedy of Massachusetts and nephew of President John F. Kennedy, was diagnosed with osteosarcoma (a form of bone cancer) in his right leg when he was twelve. Ted had some of his right leg amputated as part of this treatment. Then he became part of a clinical trial to test a new chemotherapy program that was being researched.

At that time, doctors were trying to learn how to treat osteosarcoma in young patients, and by participating in the study, Ted helped move research forward and made cures possible for many young cancer patients who came after him.

Treatments have become much more successful since Ted faced osteosarcoma in the 1970s. At that time, his chance of being cured was only 10 to 15 percent. But because of the research like the trial that he participated in, a young person diagnosed with osteosarcoma today has a chance of being cured in the 60 to 70 percent range.[25]

School isn't easy at the best of times, and you may find it really wipes you out. Go easy on yourself at first. Don't try to jump back in with all the same activities you were doing before. You may have to ease back into your old life.

Peter

I had just started college when I got cancer. I tried to go back when I was twenty, and then I stopped. I went back home, but then I decided I couldn't sit around and wait. I started technical college, but I needed surgery at the beginning of one semester and at the end of the next. I hadn't waited long enough. I wanted to move forward with my life, but I wasn't being allowed to.

My feeling then was that my life was derailed and out of control. It makes you feel helpless. But that never lasted long.

Now I'm back in college, and I'm a few years older than some people. That makes it difficult to relate at times. In some ways I look on this as my second chance, but the hard part is that I've realized I didn't necessarily have my first chance. I'm trying to do everything as right as I can, and that puts a lot of pressure on me.

> ☑ **Your teachers and your classmates want to help, so don't be afraid to ask.**

When I'm in class and people are screwing around, that really makes me mad. I have nothing against the other kids, but they haven't been through what I've been through. I definitely have a lot more sense of drive, and I know what I want to do.

Given what I've been through, the big thing for me is getting into a career where I can use my life experience as a benefit. Majoring in health psychology takes me full circle. A good education will put me in a position where I can be helping people deal with things I know about firsthand, and that I know I could be satisfied doing.[26]

* * *

SCHOLARSHIPS

There are a number of scholarships that are available to young cancer survivors. You will want to explore these options and take advantage of everything you can. There is a section in the resources that lists organizations that offer scholarships to students who currently have or have had cancer.

NOTES

1. Benjamin Disraeli, "Benjamin Disraeli Quotes," ThinkExist. com, thinkexist.com/quotation/there_is_no_education_like/192104 .html (accessed January 3, 2010).

2. Libby Falck, interview with author, July 11, 2008.

3. Juliette Walker, interview with author, September 7, 2008.

4. Powell's Books, "Synopses and Reviews: *Side Effects* by Amy Goldman Koss," www.powells.com/biblio?PID=26825&cgi=product &isbn=1596432942 (accessed March 23, 2010).

5. Justin Thomas, interview with author, December 15, 2009.

6. Jennifer Barret, "Healing Power of Yoga," *Yoga Journal*, May 2010, pp. 120–121.

7. National Cancer Institute, "Psychological Stress and Cancer: Questions and Answers," reviewed April 29, 2008, www.cancer.gov/cancertopics/factsheet/Risk/stress (accessed March 23, 2010).

8. ClinicalTrials.gov, "Effects of Tibetan Yoga on Fatigue and Sleep in Cancer," updated December 2, 2009, clinicaltrials.gov/ct2/show/NCT00507923 (accessed March 23, 2010).

9. Daily News Central, "Yoga Study Shows Benefits for Breast Cancer Patients," Health News, June 5, 2006, health.dailynewscentral.com/content/view/0002281/35/ (accessed March 23, 2010).

10. University of Texas M.D. Anderson Cancer Center, "M.D. Anderson Receives 4.5 Million Grant, Largest Ever for Study of Yoga and Cancer," Newswise, April 4, 2010, www.newswise.com/articles/md-anderson-receives-4-5-million-grant-largest-ever-for-study-of-yoga-and-cancer?ret=/articles/list&channel=&category=audiovideo&page=4&search[status]=3&search[sort]=date+desc&search[has_multimedia]=1 (accessed December 7, 2010).

11. Brittany Hill, interview with author, December 21, 2009.

12. Dr. Diane M. Puccetti, associate professor, School of Medicine and Public Health, University of Wisconsin–Madison, interview with author, August 5, 2008.

13. *Long-Term and Late Effects of Treatment for Childhood Leukemia or Lymphoma*, Informational Pamphlet No. 15, The Leukemia and Lymphoma Society, Information Resource Center, White Plains, New York, 2008.

14. Peter Williamson, "Neuropsychological Testing" (presentation at American Family Children's Hospital, 1675 Highland Avenue, Madison, Wisconsin, July 21, 2009).

15. Amber Luchterhand, interview with author, December 4, 2009.

16. Amanda Nicholls, interview with author, December 13, 2009.

17. National Cancer Institute, "Youth Smoking," *Cancer Trends Progress Report—2009/2010 Update*, progressreport.cancer.gov/doc_detail.asp?pid=1&did=2007&chid=71&coid=702&mid (accessed March 23, 2010).

18. National Children's Cancer Society, *The Mountain You Have Climbed: A Young Adult's Guide to Childhood Cancer Survivorship: Beyond the Cure*, p. 10, www.nationalchildrenscancersociety.org/NetCommunity/Document.Doc?id=51 (accessed March 22, 2010).

19. "Tobacco Use in the Pediatric and Adolescent Cancer Survivor," *Journal of Oncology Practice* 5, no. 1 (January 2009): 29.

20. "Tobacco Use in the Pediatric and Adolescent Cancer Survivor," 29.

21. "Tobacco Use in the Pediatric and Adolescent Cancer Survivor," 29.

22. "Tobacco Use in the Pediatric and Adolescent Cancer Survivor," 30.

23. National Institute on Drug Abuse for Teens, "Mind over Matter: Tobacco Addiction," NIDA for Teens, teens.drugabuse.gov/mom/mom_nic3.php (accessed March 23, 2010).

24. Seth Paulson, interview with author, December 4, 2009.

25. Dana-Farber Cancer Institute, "Personal Profiles: Edward Kennedy Jr.," www.dana-farber.org/pat/patientprofiles/personalprofiles/edwardkennedy.asp (accessed March 23, 2010).

26. Peter Greenwood, interview with author, August 20, 2008.

RESOURCES

You can listen to this podcast made on August 22, 2007, on how to balance school and cancer.

www.cancer.net/patient/Library/Podcasts/Just_for_Teens_Cancer_and_School.mp3

Teens Living with Cancer is a great website with a section all about going back to school.

www.teenslivingwithcancer.org/i-can-deal-with-it/school-issues/going-back-to-school/

American Cancer Society offers information for returning to school after being diagnosed with cancer.

www.cancer.org/Treatment/ChildrenandCancer/WhenYourChildHasCancer/children-diagnosed-with-cancer-returning-to-school

The Lance Armstrong Foundation has some information written for parents, which can also help teachers understand what you are going through and how to help you get back on track at school. You can take charge of your situation by offering this booklet to your teachers.

www.leukemia-lymphoma.org/attachments/National/br_
1139926622.pdf

Starlight Foundation has developed a DVD, *Back to School*, to
help teens like you return to school after a long absence. You
can order this free DVD on the Starlight website.

www.starlight.org/backtoschool/

Cancervive has a book, *Making the Grade: Back to School after
Cancer for Teens*, which you can order from the Cancervive
website.

www.cancervive.org/dvd.html

Scholarships

Many scholarships are available to help students who are
coping with cancer and its aftermath. Below you will find a list
of some opportunities. Many have downloadable applications.

American Cancer Society has a youth scholarship program.

ww2.cancer.org/docroot/COM/content/div_OH/COM_6_1_
Scholarship.asp

SuperSibs! has a scholarship program for siblings of cancer
patients.

www.supersibs.org/programs-and-services/scholarship-
program-main.html

The Smart Student Guide to Financial Aid lists many
scholarship options.

www.finaid.org/scholarships/cancer.phtml

Legacy of Hope is a nonprofit organization that helps
postsecondary students with financial aid.

www.stmfoundation.org/otherscholarships.html

Beyond the Cure provides information for survivors of childhood cancer, including scholarship information.

www.beyondthecure.org/future/Scholarship.pdf

The Ulman Cancer Fund for Young Adults provides scholarships.

www.ulmanfund.org/UniversityOutreach/ CollegeScholarshipProgram/tabid/686/Default.aspx

Fighting Cancer as a Volunteer

8

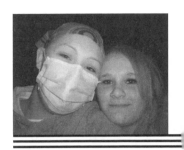

If cancer makes you feel mad, sad, or powerless because you or someone you love is fighting to live, you can do something about it. You can make a difference.

Volunteers save lives. There are fund-raising organizations out there that support research for the future and also help patients who need practical help right now. Some are giant organizations that span the globe and others do their good work in one backyard. There is a place for you to fit in.

What are you doing today? Put your talents to work for the good of others. Get involved, and you can both serve and lead. You might volunteer to stuff envelopes or organize a cartwheel-a-thon.

"Every holiday season, my family and I always go back to the hospital where I was treated for leukemia when I was little," says Jon Michael Gabrielson, who survived childhood

Never doubt that a small group of thoughtful, committed people can change the world. Indeed, it is the only thing that ever has!

—Anthropologist Margaret Mead[1]

 KICK IT

Kick It is a fund-raising organization that grew out of Flashes of Hope. You can learn about Flashes in chapter 5, "Mirror, Mirror on the Wall."

The fund-raisers are kickball games, and the money they raise goes to CureSearch[2] and the Children's Oncology Group—a network of more than five thousand doctors, nurses, and scientists who have turned childhood cancer from an almost incurable disease to one with an overall 78 percent cure rate.

You can kick it in your backyard or maybe get your school involved.[3]

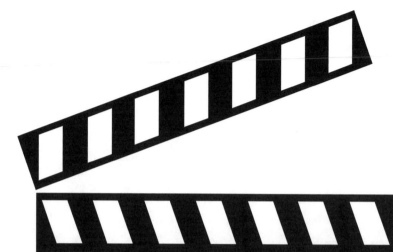

GOOD FILM: *Cancer Stories*

After her own experience with cancer, art teacher and video producer Nancy Hamilton Myers put together profiles of people who have also battled the disease—and relied on their Christian faith throughout the ordeal. The stories are as varied as the people telling them and include a NASA engineer, a star athlete, children, mothers, fathers, and more, each navigating the challenges of the disease in his or her own courageous way.

Nancy has gathered together stories from people who have found the strength to face cancer through their Christian faith. This film features people confronting cancer with courage and dignity.

This is a film packed with very real, firsthand accounts. It approaches cancer from both a personal and medical perspective. It is focused on providing comfort and encouragement to people who are battling cancer and also speaks to their loved ones.

You can get this film at Gateway Films' website, www .visionvideo.com/detail.taf?_function=detail&a_product_ id=34725.

leukemia and is an English major in college now. "I remember being stuck in the hospital during the holidays. I remember how much better it made me feel as a kid when people would donate things."[4]

Cancer is expensive. The medical bills pile up fast for a family that is fighting cancer. Cancer research is also costly. The U.S. government has poured more than $75 billion into

GOOD FILM: *The Truth about Cancer*

Using her husband's struggle with cancer as a case in point, filmmaker Linda Garmon explores his fight against the devastating disease and also spotlights the lives of the medical professionals dedicated to curing it, interweaving personal testimony with science.

What is the truth about cancer? This ninety-minute documentary looks at what we know and also what we don't know yet about how to fight cancer. It follows several medical professionals researching the latest developments in cancer treatment as well as helping patients and their families live with a diagnosis of cancer.

The conclusion of this compelling documentary puts it on the line as breast cancer survivor and broadcast journalist Linda Ellerbee moderates a dialogue between doctors who have all had cancer themselves. These panelists know what they are talking about when they discuss how to handle a cancer diagnosis, what to say to your loved ones, how to advocate for yourself, and how best to live your life with cancer.

research since our government declared war on cancer in 1971. The big pharmaceutical companies have spent even more.[5]

Cancer organizations are all scrambling to get the money they must spend to provide the services people need while they are fighting cancer. You can help them. Look for events in your area that you can plug into. You'll find a list of national organizations in the resources section at the end of this chapter. Some of these groups work specifically with teens and for teens.

Take part in a fund-raiser, and get your friends to come with you. Maybe you can put up posters or hand out flyers or e-mail to let people know about a cancer fund-raising event.

To find out the best place you can fit in as a volunteer, you need to find a way to match your personality and skills with the needs in your area. The National Cancer Institute has created a guide to help you make the best choice.[6]

If two or more statements below describe you, then you may want to work with cancer service and support organizations.

- I like to meet new people.
- I like to listen to others.
- I like to share information I know about cancer with others.
- I want to help people who are coping with cancer.
- People helped me while I was in cancer treatment, and now I want to help people who are going through treatment.

You may even want to start your own support group. Libby Falck put together a support group from the friends she made at cancer camp called Teens Tackling Cancer. "We are a small group of kids in Wisconsin and Illinois. We help each other with our treatments, and we plan events together like horseback riding. It brings people together outside of camp and is another opportunity to socialize outside the hospital."[7]

Brittany Hill has used her experience with cancer to help others. "My school had a blood drive. They weren't getting many donors. So I told my story and shared my pictures, and two hundred people signed up," she says. "I didn't need the blood myself, but I wanted to give back to people who had cancer right now."

"I like to talk to schools and with other people who are going through the same thing I did," Brittany continues. "I tell about my experience, and how I pulled through. They gave me twenty-four hours to live, and yet here I am four years later. I want to give people hope."[9]

☑ **THE ULMAN CANCER FUND FOR YOUNG ADULTS**

The Ulman Cancer Fund for Young Adults is a leading voice in the young adult cancer movement. It works to raise awareness about the young adult cancer issue and make sure all young adults and their families have what they need to thrive. They organize events you may want to get involved in.[8]

WRISTBANDS BUILD CANCER AWARENESS

These gel bracelets are known as awareness bracelets. When you wear a colored silicone wristband, you are generating funds that support cancer research and let everyone around you know what is important to you. The most recognized example is the yellow LIVESTRONG wristband that shows you support cancer awareness and research.

The LIVESTRONG band is part of the Wear Yellow and Live Strong educational program organized by the Lance Armstrong Foundation to raise cancer awareness and encourage everyone to live life to the fullest. When he was twenty-five, Lance was diagnosed with testicular cancer that had spread to his lungs and brain. After chemotherapy, he went on to win the 1999 Tour de France and won it for six years in a row.[10]

The Lance Armstrong Foundation chose yellow because it is an important color in Lance's field—bicycling. The yellow jersey is worn by the leader of the Tour de France, a garment that Lance has practically worn out. When Lance appeared on *The Colbert Report*, Steven Colbert helped promote the wristband through humor by wearing a band he had made that said "Wriststrong."[11]

The LIVESTRONG wristbands have inspired a whole family of wristbands. Pink bands are used to remind people of the war against breast cancer that is being waged every day. Bracelets supporting pancreatic cancer awareness and research are purple.[12]

Wristbands have been used by many people who want to let the world know what they care about. April Winchell—famous voice actress who has been heard on programs including *King of the Hill, The Simpsons, Beverly Hills Chihuahua, Toy Story 2, The Lion King,* and *Beauty and the Beast*—followed Lance's model and created a wristband as part of her own battle with cancer. Her wristbands glow in the dark.

Gel wristbands are about making a statement. You can probably find one to support the cause of your choice by searching the website or a supporting organization. Wear one and share one.

"SMILES OF HOPE," AN ESSAY BY JULIETTE WALKER

Juliette Walker wrote a speech about her experience with cancer. "My speech is about presenting the gift of hope to other kids who have cancer. It felt good to bring my experience into my speech. I had a running metaphor, and it was smiling. Even during the sad parts of my experience with cancer, I found reasons to smile, and I listed the reasons."[13]

Everyone can smile. We might find it hard to smile sometimes, especially when we feel like crying, but even through those times in our lives, we can find a reason to smile.

I was once in your shoes, and I know how terribly alone and scared you can feel when you are diagnosed with cancer. Know that there are many other teenagers who are battling cancer just like you are. It is ok to feel scared, but also know that there is hope. There is a reason to smile through all this uncertainty.

This past November I had a cancerous tumor removed, and before I could think about what had happened I started a short, intense schedule of chemotherapy. I was very fortunate. The cancer had not spread, and the chemo was just a precaution to make sure it didn't spread. That was one reason I had to smile, one reason I could hope and know that I was going to get out just fine.

Though our situations may be completely different, I know that cancer is a time in our lives when we feel confused and lost. You probably have many questions that not even the doctors can answer. Only time can answer them.

When I was first told I was going to have to have chemo, I thought the worst part was going to be losing my hair. It was a reminder that my body was being put under so much pressure by the drugs. But I did find a few things to smile about. I got many very cute hats as gifts, I didn't have to shave my legs, and when I was up on the oncology ward it didn't even matter that I didn't have hair, because all the other kids didn't have hair too!

The tolls that the chemo took on my body were very devastating. But by the time I finished my third round of in-patient chemo, it was encouraging to see myself improving so much, and it was very encouraging for my friends to see as well.

Let your friends help you. If you have been recently diagnosed, chances are, the people finding out about you are very sad or shocked. It is very hard to see people that you love reacting this way, but if you are able to show them a positive attitude, it won't be long before your attitude rubs off on them. It is amazing how much support friends, family, neighbors, classmates, teachers, and teammates can offer. Put a smile on your face. Show them your courage. That's how you can help them.

I hope today you were able to receive my gift. It can't really be touched or held, but it can be felt. So look at the person sitting next to you, and smile. We are put into each others lives to encourage one another. So I will leave you with my gift and my last words—never stop hoping and never stop smiling.

You might like to work with a cancer-awareness organization if you like to

- teach people about cancer,
- speak in front of groups of people, and
- talk about issues that are important to you, like cancer screening or support for people with cancer.

Jon Michael used his cancer experience to get involved with politics in his community. "My senior year in high school, no one was running against the mayor of Appleton, and I didn't think that was fair, so I ran as a write-in candidate," he says. "It was a small thing at school, but somehow the news media got hold of it, and it became a big deal in the TV and newspaper, and it prompted more people to jump into the race. It brought interest in politics back to Appleton, and I ended up getting nine percent of the vote."

"People knew who I was because I was known for my leukemia," Jon Michael explains, "and I decided to do something good with that. Actually I defaulted into a lot of leadership positions. I always stepped into lead even though I was really shy before the leukemia. I didn't talk to anybody before I got cancer, but then I had to talk to a lot of adults, and that's how I learned my social skills—in the hospital."[15]

Seth Paulson volunteers for A Whole New Ballgame, an organization that helps students with disabilities who are entering the technical college he attends. Seth advises new students on how to cope. There may be a place where you would fit in as a volunteer in your school too.

> ☑ **NATIONAL COALITION FOR CANCER SURVIVORSHIP**
>
> This group of cancer survivors is speaking out on issues that you care about. National Coalition for Cancer Survivorship helps survivors speak up for themselves to lawmakers and policy makers to make the path through cancer easier. They offer a cancer advo-kit to help you get started making your voice heard.
>
> Advocacy doesn't have to be hard or take a lot of time. There are many ways you can act from your own home. One way is to share your story with your legislators by letter, e-mail, or phone. The National Coalition for Cancer Survivorship can show you how.[14]

You might like to work on a special fund-raising event if you like to

- ◎ **work with people and be part of large events,**
- ◎ **help with a local event near where you live, and**
- ◎ **want to get involved, but can only help once in a while.**

Cancer survivor Kenzie Derr worked on Relay for Life at her school. "This year I'm in charge of the survivorship committee. I love to meet other survivors and hear their stories," Kenzie says. "Our school was number one in the nation for raising money. I'm proud of that fact. I like being involved with Relay for Life and doing car washes and things like that."[16]

Everyone knows about benefit concerts organized by celebrities. But you don't have to be a celebrity to organize a benefit concert. Justin Thomas did a benefit concert at his college with his band, *Syncere*, and dedicated the proceeds to Camp Smile-a-Mile. "Our audience was college students," says Justin, "so we didn't want to make the admission too high. We charged two dollars or one dollar with a canned good. We donated half the proceeds to Camp Smile-a-Mile and half to local charity kitchens. It wasn't a large sum of money, but I think they appreciated it."[18]

RELAY FOR LIFE

Many communities use this fun-filled overnight event designed to celebrate survivorship and raise money for research and programs of the American Cancer Society. It has spread to twenty-one countries. At a relay, teams of volunteers take turns walking or running laps and try to keep at least one team member on the track at all times.

By participating in the relay, you will be helping to raise money for cancer research and cancer patients and to spread the word about cancer awareness, celebrate the lives of survivors, and remember those who have lost their lives to cancer. You can volunteer for a team or become a team captain. Captains recruit walkers and runners. The captains are the heart and soul of the event.[17]

When Jon Michael was a senior in high school, he organized a concert for his children's hospital. "They used to have concerts at my high school," Jon Michael remembers, "so I just brought it back. I planned it, and my band played for it. All the money we raised was sent to a children's fund to help out with the hospital. That was the most proud moment of my life—giving back."[19]

4PeteSake is a local fund-raiser that was started to help out Peter, a teen in Spring Green, Wisconsin, who lost his leg to bone cancer. After helping Peter, 4PeteSake has developed a life

Peter's band playing at a fund-raiser. *Courtesy of Peter Greenwood.*

of its own. "We started this because my insurance originally wouldn't pay for the prosthesis that made the most sense for me to have because I was a younger person," says Peter. "I needed one with a computer in the knee so I could be more active. My town started this fund-raiser four summers ago, and they raised enough money to get my prosthesis. Now the money they raise goes to other needy people in the community."[20]

Getting involved in service or fund-raising for a cause you believe in can surprise you. You probably signed on because you wanted to do something good for others, but you will find that volunteering gives you a positive feeling about yourself as well.

Volunteering and fund-raising can be really fun—even the hardest parts. You will walk away feeling like you really accomplished something, and that gives you quite a lift.

MICE CONTRIBUTE TO CANCER RESEARCH

Twenty million mice and rats are used in research in the United States each year. Mice are the most widely used because they are small, inexpensive to raise, and easy to handle, and they also reproduce very quickly. They share 99 percent of their genes with humans, and now they can be genetically engineered and modified to make their reactions even closer to humans. That makes them a good model to study many human diseases, including cancer.[21]

The discovery of nude mice in 1962 was a major breakthrough in cancer research. The hairless mutant is also immunodeficient, which means it is less able to fight infections and other diseases, and it also means that it does not reject tumor transplants from other animals. Researchers can transplant an actual human tumor into a nude mouse and study how the animal reacts.

Today, mice can be engineered by modifying their genes to create mice to study very specific questions about how cancer works. As researchers learn more about how tumors start and grow, they can develop better treatments and cures for cancer. Also, mice with tumors have been exposed to radiation and different chemicals to see what happens to their tumors.[22]

 4PETESAKE

This local fund-raiser was started to help Peter Greenwood, a twenty-year-old bone cancer survivor with an above-the-knee amputation. To stay active, he needed one of the new generation of computer-activated prosthetic legs, but his insurance didn't cover it. People in his community decided to raise the money for it, and they ended up raising more than Pete needed for a new leg. Since then, the organization has raised nearly two hundred thousand dollars and has changed the lives of nine more people who needed help.

This is the kind of thing that can spring up in your community when people understand the need.[23]

WALKING FOR CANCER

Avon Walk for Breast Cancer raises money with a two-day walk of 39 miles. Walks take place all over the country every summer. Della Hansmann, a teen volunteer at one of these walks, tells how she took the first step:

I think I saw a postcard for the Avon Breast Cancer Walk on a table in a coffee shop and was intrigued. I took it home and thought about it, and it sounded fun. I don't think I was even really looking for a volunteer activity, but it seemed like a neat thing to do. I checked out the age requirements. You had to be sixteen, and I was turning sixteen the week before the walk, so I thought—It's fate! I think I was the youngest person on that walk.

It didn't seem like it would be that hard (although it turned out to be a little harder than I thought). You walk thirty-nine miles in two days. You were supposed to train for it for months ahead of time. They arranged local groups you could get involved with for training. But I ignored all that. I thought I was young and strong, and I could do just fine. That turned out to be not the wisest plan ever, but I did manage it.

The hardest part for me wasn't the walking—it was soliciting donations because you had to have financial sponsors. The idea is you contact friends, family, and corporations and get them to sponsor you in doing this crazy feat. I had a really hard time with that. I don't like asking for money, but I wrote letter to everyone in my extended family and went around and knocked on doors in the neighborhood. Actually everyone was happy to help. It was easier than I thought it would be, but it was still hard.

They had it all set up with stations for refreshment. They didn't want anybody getting dehydrated. They pretty much forced you to take a water or Gatorade at every stop. They had medical stations with volunteer nurses.

I met some great people on the walk. I've always been a little shy of strangers, but it was different there. You already know you're going to like almost everyone you meet. You don't know anything about them, but you do know they have volunteered to do this cool thing. It's a selector for warm-hearted people.

I would recommend this to anyone. It makes you feel good about yourself. Volunteering is supposed to be doing something for others, but you get a really positive feeling for yourself as well. I wish more people knew that. Then more people would volunteer.[24]

ALEX'S LEMONADE STAND

This foundation is committed to finding a cure for all children with cancer up to the age of twenty-one. Since Alex, a four-year-old cancer patient set up her stand in 2000, the organization has raised over $35 million, which has been used to fund research projects and help families who need to travel for treatment.

Nearly half of that money has been raised directly from lemonade stands. You can set up a stand in your school cafeteria or take it beyond your school. Go to the foundation's website (find it in the resources at the end of this chapter) and click on "Stand Central," or you can try other events like a bake sale. One group held a cartwheel-a-thon. You will be assigned a stand coach to help you with the details.[25]

NOTES

1. Margaret Mead, "Margaret Mead Quotes," Brainy Quote, www.brainyquote.com/quotes/authors/m/margaret_mead.html (accessed January 3, 2010).

2. CureSearch, "About Us," www.curesearch.org/about_us/index.aspx (accessed January 3, 2010).

3. Kick It, www.kick-it.org/ (accessed January 3, 2010).

4. Jon Michael Gabrielson, interview with author, December 7, 2009.

5. Catherine Arnst, "Cancer's Cruel Economics," *Business Week*, May 21, 2008, www.businessweek.com/magazine/content/08_22/b4086000467675.htm (accessed January 3, 2010).

6. National Cancer Institute, "Finding Ways You Can Make a Difference: A Guide," *Facing Forward: Ways You Can Make a Difference in Cancer*, updated June 1, 2002, www.cancer.gov/cancertopics/make-a-difference/page3 (accessed March 24, 2010).

7. Libby Falck, interview with author, December 14, 2009.

8. The Ulman Cancer Fund for Young Adults, www.ulmanfund.org/ (accessed January 3, 2010).

9. Brittany Hill, interview with author, December 21, 2009.

10. BBC News, "What's the Yellow One For?" updated February 1, 2005 news.bbc.co.uk/cbbcnews/hi/newsid_4220000/newsid_4226500/4226551.stm (accessed March 24, 2010).

11. Wikipedia, "Livestrong Wristband," updated March 20, 2010, http://en.wikipedia.org/wiki/Livestrong_wristband (accessed March 24, 2010).

12. Wikipedia, "Gel Bracelet," updated February 27, 2010, en.wikipedia.org/wiki/Gel_bracelet (accessed March 24, 2010).

13. Juliette Walker, interview with author, September 4, 2008.

14. National Coalition for Cancer Survivorship, "What Is Advocacy?" www.canceradvocacy.org/take-action/cancer-advocacy/ (accessed January 3, 2010).

15. Gabrielson, interview.

16. Kenzie Derr, interview with author, December 21, 2009.

17. Relay for Life, "Team Captain Toolkit," www.relayforlife .org/relay/teamcaptains (accessed January 3, 2010).

18. Justin Thomas, interview with author, December 15, 2009.

19. Gabrielson, interview.

20. Peter Greenwood, interview with author, August 11, 2008.

21. Wikipedia, "Animal Testing," updated March 24, 2010, en.wikipedia.org/wiki/Animal_testing (accessed March 24, 2010).

22. Lynette A. Hart and Amy Dassler, "Mouse in Science: Cancer Research," UC Davis Center for Animal Alternatives Information, updated April 14, 2009, www.vetmed.ucdavis.edu/Animal_ Alternatives/cancer.htm (accessed March 24, 2010).

23. 4PeteSake, 4ps.qa1.compcc.com/ (accessed January 3, 2010).

24. Della Hansmann, interview with author, January 5, 2010.

25. Alex's Lemonade Stand Foundation, www.alexslemonade .org/slideshow (accessed January 3, 2010).

RESOURCES

Alex's Lemonade Stand
333 E. Lancaster Ave., #414
Wynnewood, PA 19096
866-333-1213

Alex's Lemonade Stand came into being when four-year-old Alex, who had been diagnosed with cancer at age one, set up a lemonade stand to help fund research for a cure. Using her model of grassroots fund-raising, volunteers have already raised more than $35 million for cancer research.

www.alexslemonade.org

Avon Walk for Breast Cancer

There are Avon Walk organizations in Boston, Massachusetts; Charlotte, North Carolina; Chicago, Illinois; Houston,

Texas; New York, New York; Summit County, Colorado;
San Francisco, California; Santa Barbara, California; and
Washington, D.C.

Find one near you by calling the number below.

888-540-9255

www.avonwalk.org/index.html

Candlelighters Childhood Cancer Foundation
P.O. Box 498
Kensington, Maryland 20895
800-366-2223

This group was formed under the name Candlelighters in 1970
and is now one of the largest grassroots, national organizations
dedicated to improving the lives of children and adolescents
with cancer.

www.candlelighters.org/AboutUs/AboutACCO.aspx

Kick It
6009 Landerhaven Drive, Suite 1
Cleveland, Ohio 44124
440-442-9700

Kick It uses the game of kickball as a fund-raiser. All the
proceeds go to fund research at the Children's Oncology
Group, the world's largest cooperative research organization
with a network of more than five thousand physicians, nurses,
and scientists.

www.kick-it.org/

The National Cancer Institute website has an encyclopedia
of cancer organizations. It can be a good place to start your
search.

www.cancer.gov/cancertopics/make-a-difference/page8#H5

National Coalition for Cancer Survivorship
1010 Wayne Avenue
Suite 70
Silver Spring, Maryland 20910
888-650-9127

The National Coalition for Cancer Survivorship is an organization that helps cancer survivors advocate for their own care or for the care of others. Learn how to make your voice heard in a way that makes a difference.

www.canceradvocacy.org/take-action/cancer-advocacy/

Relay for Life
800-227-2345

Each year millions of people around the world organize relays in their communities to raise the funds and awareness that can save lives. At a relay, teams take turns walking or running around a track, keeping a team member on the track at all times, including through the night because cancer never sleeps. There is a relay near you that can use your help, perhaps as a team captain.

www.relayforlife.org/relay/teamcaptains

The Ulman Cancer Fund for Young Adults
10440 Little Patuxent Parkway
Suite G1
Columbia, Maryland 21044
410-964-0402

Every young adult affected by cancer should have access to the resources they need to survive. The Ulman Cancer Fund for Young Adults is working to empower young adult cancer survivors to help themselves and help others.

www.ulmanfund.org/

9

Am I a
Survivor Yet?

You are a cancer survivor from the moment your doctor tells you that you have cancer. Some people think you can only be a survivor after you complete your treatment. Other people say that to be a survivor you must live five years after your doctor delivers the bad news. But according to the President's Cancer Panel, you are a survivor from the moment you know you have cancer, and you'll be a survivor for the rest of your life.[1]

Nobody is going to vote you off this island.

Still, most teens say they really begin to feel like survivors when their treatment is done, and they can start to put their lives back together.

Amber

You know that feeling you get when you're on a roller coaster, and it's climbing the first incline. It seems like it's NEVER going to end. Up, up, up you go. You're holding onto the bar in front of you for dear life and the "click . . . click . . . click" gets slower and slower and then, finally, it stops. That's when you know you're going for the ride of your life.

That's the feeling I have right now. For five years I've been climbing that immeasurable incline and my "click . . . click . . . clicks" are finally coming to an end. I've been holding onto that safety bar and shaking it to make sure it's REALLY locked. I've looked down in horror at the terrible distance I have put between me and the precious ground, and I've thought to myself, "How

I'm just twenty years old. I don't have all the answers. I survived this disease, but there is more to me than that. One of the hardest things is trying to decide who I am without cancer. All my life I've been defined as the girl with cancer. Who is Libby?

—Libby Falck, twenty, diagnosed with bone cancer at age five[2]

did I get here? Can you PLEASE stop this ride and let me off, because I'm totally not ready for this!"

But there's no turning back. I know I can't stop this ride.

My whole life has been leading up to this moment. I know there will be other hills to climb, but this one is something special. I'm on the downward slope, and for once in my life, that's a good thing! Four and a half weeks, people! So I'm having a party. I know. I had an "off treatment" party last time. (Because we all know how that turned out.) But I've decided that this REALLY deserves a party. So we're calling this my "off treatment FOR GOOD" party, or my "never going back" party, or "bye-bye Baldie" party, or something. Who knows? EVERYONE is invited. I don't care who you are![3]

*   *   *

As a survivor, you are in the same great, big boat with more than 10 million other cancer survivors in the United States,

AVOID SOLVENTS LINKED TO CANCER

Some of the solvents used in paint thinners, paint and grease removers, and in dry cleaning are known or suspected of causing cancer in animal studies. A solvent is a substance that can dissolve another substance and, so, always needs to be handled with care.

The ones you particularly want to avoid include benzene, carbon tetrachloride, chloroform, dichloromethane, and trichloroethylene. Probably the simplest way to be safe is watch out for big words on the label. If you are suspicious, Google it, and get the facts.

Benzene is known to cause leukemia in humans. It has widespread use in the chemical and drug industries and as a component of gasoline. Since 1997, it has been banned as an ingredient in pesticides. Inhaling contaminated air is the primary way you can be exposed to benzene. You will be breathing it around gas stations and in areas with a lot of auto exhaust. It is also part of cigarette smoke. About half of the exposure to benzene in the United States is from cigarette smoking. It's hard to keep auto exhaust out of our lungs, but we all have control over how much cigarette smoke we inhale.[4]

according to the American Cancer Society.[5] But if you were diagnosed between the ages of fifteen and twenty-nine, you are dealing with a special set of issues. The President's Cancer Panel calls you the "orphaned cohort."[6] Cohort means a group of people who are being followed in a scientific study, but not that many people have been studying you. When scientists want to see what research has been done on a topic, they go to the National Library of Medicine's PubMed database, but less than 1 percent of the cancer-related articles listed there for the years 1993 to 2003 were specifically about adolescents and young adults. Most of the time, information about you has been filed away as part of a much larger group labeled Cancer Survivors Diagnosed in Childhood.[7]

One reason for the "orphan" status is that it can be tricky for researchers to keep track of teens and young adults. You often move away from the place where you got treatment to go to college or chase a job or see the world. People who study cancer are realizing that your cohort needs its share of the research pie, and they have learned a lot lately thanks to the generosity of hundreds of young cancer survivors who have filled out long surveys and shared their lives in a huge project called "The Childhood Cancer Survivor Study." More than fourteen thousand cancer survivors who were diagnosed before the age of twenty-one have now been studied for over five years. The same study also looked at 3,700 brothers and sisters of young people with cancer and compared their health with the cancer survivors. A second long-term survey is now under way because changes in cancer treatments will mean changing long-term effects for survivors.[8]

GOOD NEWS–BAD NEWS

One in every 350 people will develop cancer before the age of twenty, but in the 1950s scientists would not have been able to do "The Childhood Cancer Survivor Study" because they wouldn't have had enough survivors to study.

Back then very few children survived cancer. Today, treatments like chemotherapy and radiation therapy make it possible for eight out of ten young people who get cancer to be long-term survivors.[9] However, these amazing treatments are like a good news–bad news joke, and the bad news is that the same treatments that stopped the growth of cancer can lead to an ominous outcome called *late effects*.

LATE EFFECTS OF CANCER

When cancer cells were destroyed by your treatment, healthy cells that your body needs were also destroyed. As a result, you may suffer from late effects of cancer. Studies indicate that more than two-thirds of young adult survivors of childhood cancer eventually suffer at least one late effect. Not all survivors have to deal with serious late effects, but you will need to pay extra attention to your health from now on.[10]

Because cancer cells are growing out of control, treatments that can stop them may also stop other cells that are naturally multiplying fast as a part of your growth process. Treatments aimed at rapidly growing cells hit childhood cancer survivors especially hard because when you are a child, your bones, organs, and other tissues are all growing fast, and the cancer treatment can prevent them from growing normally.

Late effects are like land mines that you are going to have to be watching for the rest of your life. The treatments that stopped your cancer may well affect your brain, eyes, ears, organs, bones, and reproductive system. You may have to deal with learning disabilities, memory loss, anxiety, depression, obesity, and even more cancers. "The Childhood Cancer Survivor Study" found that six out of ten survivors had at least one chronic health condition and almost three out of ten had a serious or life-threatening condition. Survivors are ten times more likely to deal with learning problems, fifteen times more likely to have congestive heart failure or to develop a second cancer, and fifty-four times more likely to have a major joint replacement than their brothers and sisters who have not had cancer.[11]

It is important for you to know what to expect. Late effects can show up in everything from your organs and bones to your moods, feelings, thinking, learning, and memory.

Remember, not everyone experiences late effects. The risk that your cancer treatment will cause late effects depends on many things, including

- ◎ **the type of cancer you had and where it was in your body,**
- ◎ **your age when treated,**
- ◎ **the type and amount of treatment,**
- ◎ **the area treated, and**
- ◎ **genetic factors or health problems you had before the cancer.**

Late effects of radiation therapy are rare, but they do happen. Here's an idea of what to look for:

Brain changes: Radiation therapy to the brain can cause problems that appear months or years after your treatment ends. Side effects can include memory loss, problems doing math, movement problems, trouble thinking, or personality changes.

Infertility: For men, infertility means not being able to get a woman pregnant. For women, it means not being able to get pregnant. This does not mean that you cannot become a parent, but infertility is something you need to discuss with your doctor.

Joint changes: Radiation therapy can cause scar tissue and weakness in the part of the body that was treated. This can lead to loss of motion in your joints, such as your jaw, shoulders, or hips. Joint problems might show up months or years after radiation therapy is complete. You need to be aware of early signs of joint problems. They could include trouble getting your mouth to open wide or pain when you make certain movements, such as reaching over your head or putting your hand in a back pocket. If you experience these side effects, your doctor may refer you to a physical therapist who can give you exercises to help you have less pain and improve your movement.

Lymphedema: This is swelling in your arm or leg caused by a buildup of lymph fluid. You may be at risk if your lymph nodes were removed during surgery or damaged by radiation therapy. Tell your doctor if you notice swelling in your arm or leg on the side where you had radiation therapy. Some early symptoms are pain or a sense of heaviness in your arm or leg and a feeling of tightness or weakness in your arm or leg. Exercise can help prevent and treat lymphedema.

Justin, now pursuing theater instead of sports. *Courtesy of Justin Thomas.*

Mouth changes: If you had radiation therapy to your head and neck, you need to watch for late effects in your mouth, which could include dry mouth, cavities, or bone loss in your jaw. As a cancer survivor, you need to have your teeth checked every one to two months for at least six months after radiation treatment. You also need to take extra good care of your teeth and gums—this means flossing, using daily fluoride treatments, and brushing your teeth after meals and before you go to bed.

Secondary cancer: Radiation therapy can cause a new cancer many years after you have finished treatment. This does not happen often, but you need to have check-ups for the rest of your life to watch for any new cancer that might occur.[12]

Researchers and doctors are constantly looking for treatments that reduce late effects, but as a cancer survivor, you are part of high-risk population. You are going to need long-term (translate: lifelong) follow-up.

PHYSICAL SURVIVORSHIP

Most teens with cancer are treated in children's hospitals. So, besides taking charge of your own survivorship when you move away from home, you will also need to switch to doctors who treat adults. This means that you will suddenly be dealing with a medical system that expects you to be your own advocate.

When you are finally feeling better, you may not like to talk about cancer or even think about it, but understanding your survivorship and taking charge of it is the next step.

Peggy Possin, coordinator of the Long-Term Survival Clinic at the University Hospital and Pediatric Specialties Clinic in Madison, Wisconsin, tells the teens who attend her survival clinics,

You are going to be in college in a few years. You are going to get sick, and you are going to go to urgent care, and you need to say to the person who comes through the door, "I am here because I had leukemia," or "I'm here because I had my spleen taken out as part of my therapy for cancer, so I just want you to know that." People won't know it by looking at you, but these are things they need to know. You worked really hard to get healthy, and we want to keep you healthy.[13]

You probably received a big binder of information while you were in therapy. Your parents may have taken charge of it and carried it everywhere. It's your binder now. It's a kind of parachute to help you avoid a crash landing as you transition from frequent visits with nice familiar stuff like lab work, x-rays, scans, and tests to what is sometimes called (but actually never is) normal life. When you reach the end of treatment, it is a time for celebration. It's also time for you to take the controls.

If you had cancer when you were really young, it is even more important for you dig back into the details of that experience now that you are taking charge of your own life. Studies show that a lot of survivors who had cancer as children don't have a clear idea of exactly what type of cancer they had or how it was treated. This is information you must make sure you have.

> ☑ **PESTICIDES LINKED TO CANCER**
>
> **Since World War Two, Americans have been using more and more pesticides to grow more food and to create pretty yards, parks, and golf courses. Nearly nine hundred active ingredients are registered as pesticides in the United States. So far about twenty of them have been linked to cancer, and many more may be once they are tested.[14]**
>
> **It's a good idea to get your hands on organic food when you can. This will help you to lower your exposure to chemicals that may cause cancer.**

Libby

My doctor and I have been talking about how to transition. Right now I have literally a four-foot stack of files from all the cancer years. I think what I'm going to do with that is put it on a mini DVD and keep it with me. There's a lot, but you can make a short list of what you need to watch for—like heart problems. I'm prone to certain diseases from the chemos I was on.[15]

(Libby was diagnosed with bone cancer in her right leg at age five, and seven years later she was diagnosed with a different kind of bone cancer in the same place, which may have been caused by the original radiation treatment.)

*   *   *

MEDICAL RECORDS AND FOLLOW-UP CARE

Be sure to ask your oncologist for a written summary of your treatment. In the summary, he or she can suggest what aspects of your health need to be followed. Then share this summary with any new doctors you see, especially your primary care doctor, as you discuss your follow-up care plan.

Many people keep their medical records in a binder or folder and refer to them as they see new doctors. This keeps key facts about your cancer treatment in the same place. Other kinds of health information you should keep include

the date you were diagnosed;
the type of cancer you were treated for;
pathology reports that describe the type and stage of cancer;
places and dates of specific treatment, such as details of all surgeries, sites and total amounts of radiation therapy, names and doses of chemotherapy and all other drugs, and key lab reports, x-ray reports, CT scans, and MRI reports;
list of signs to watch for and possible long-term effects of treatment;
contact information for all health professionals involved in your treatments and follow-up care;
any problems that occurred during or after treatment; and
information about supportive care you received (such as special medicines, emotional support, and nutritional supplements).

Be sure to give any new doctors that you see a copy of your treatment summary or medical records.[16]

Peter

I'm just hitting that two-year mark so I need to take care of that and get it sorted out. Off the top of my head I can remember just about every chemo I had. They gave me so many different drugs at one point or another and so many surgeries. Part of me is probably subconsciously letting it slide because I don't feel like I want to remember it. I know the records are accessible. I've got the scars to remind me.[17]

* * *

ECONOMIC SURVIVORSHIP—YOUR JOB HUNT

What do you want to be when you grow up? This is a question adults have probably been pestering you with. But haven't you been asking yourself the same thing? Being a cancer survivor will have an impact on your answer. The President's Cancer Panel warns that you may be facing a tougher road to self-sufficiency than your friends who are not cancer survivors.

Since you have been battling cancer, coping with treatments, and trying to keep up in school, you may find your work résumé is a little thin compared to classmates who aren't cancer survivors. The playing field gets even smaller if you now have a disability or other aftereffects of cancer or its treatment that mean you need special accommodations in the workplace. On top of that, as a young survivor looking for a job, some employers may be scared away if you tell them you are a cancer survivor.

The Americans with Disabilities Act and the Federal Rehabilitation Act can give you some protection from job discrimination because you have had cancer. Under federal law, an employer with fifteen or more employees cannot treat you differently from other workers because of a cancer history, as long as you are qualified for the job. Also, a prospective employer is not allowed to ask you about your health history during an interview unless he or she sees you have a disability that might interfere with you performing the duties of the job.

Many young cancer survivors find that when they start to look at career choices, the time they have spent with people in the medical profession powerfully influences their job choices. After experiencing the good that can be done by caring members of their medical team, many set their sights on a career in medicine and can often feel more certain of their direction than do their classmates who have not faced life-threatening illness. You could look at this as one possible silver lining of the cancer cloud.

IONIZING RADIATION LINKED TO CANCER

Ionizing radiation can damage your genes in ways that are linked to cancer. We are all exposed to small doses of ionizing radiation from cosmic rays that enter earth's atmosphere from outer space. However we may be more at risk from radiation coming out of the ground in the form of radon.

Radon happens when uranium in the ground breaks down. Certain types of rocky soil have more radon than others. Radon gas seeps into homes through cracks and other openings in the house foundation. About one out of twenty homes has levels of radon that are considered dangerous. This radon has been linked to twenty thousand lung cancer deaths every year in the United States. If you live in an area where radon levels are considered high, you should ask your parents to have your house tested and, if necessary, look into ways to lower your radon exposure.

Fallout, the radioactive material released by atomic bombs, is also linked to cancer. The survivors of the atomic bombs dropped on Japan during World War Two have had increased risks of leukemia and cancers of the breast, thyroid, lung, stomach, and other organs. Radioactive substances were also released in above-ground atomic bomb testing conducted by the U.S. government in this country in the late 1950s and early 1960s in Nevada.

If you are a cancer patient, you may well have been exposed to ionizing radiation as part of your therapy. Some patients who receive radiation treatments for cancer may be at increased risk for more cancer. If you have had radiation therapy, it is important to let every new doctor who treats you know about it.[18]

Amber

I really want to go to nursing school. When I was sick all my nurses were a source of encouragement. Because I was in a children's hospital, the nurses connected with me because I was closer to their age. They spent a lot of time with me. They really became my friends. I appreciated that and want to do the same for other people. I had one nurse who had cancer when she was a senior in high school, and she could really relate to me. She really helped me through.[19]

Juliette

I'm not really sure what major I want to do in college, but after going through all this stuff at the hospital, it kind of makes me want to explore a career in medicine. I'm not sure about being a doctor. All the doctors I had were very compassionate and had a passion for what they were doing. All the nurses I had—I really loved them. They seem to really love what they are doing. It would be rewarding to be able to help people the way they helped me.[20]

* * *

INSURING YOUR FUTURE

Everyone needs health insurance, but as a cancer survivor, you should be at the front of the line because you can expect to need follow-up care related to your treatment. Unfortunately, as you "age out" of your parents' insurance, you may well find yourself uninsured. Your parents' insurance company will usually drop you when you reach a certain age (or age out). The point at which you age out can vary, depending on what state you live in.

According to the U.S. Census Bureau statistics from 2002, people eighteen to twenty-four are least likely to have insurance. The fact that young adults tend not to be able to find insurance is part of the reason why you belong to the "orphaned cohort" of people who have not been studied. The sad fact is that so few young people can afford medical treatment, and therefore, they provide few medical records for researchers to study.

You will need to create a team of adults who can help you explore your options in Medicare and Medicaid, health insurance you can get through government assistance. Insurance coverage may also influence your choice of jobs. Employment in government and with established companies often provides better insurance options for cancer survivors.

Peter

One of the harder things is insurance. It's frustrating. In some ways I'm trapped on welfare. I would be fine if they would just let me have the insurance and let me work. I want to generate my own income. But right now I need to get an education and then I'll find a job that comes with insurance.[21]

* * *

EMOTIONAL SURVIVORSHIP

The late effects land mines that can affect your body can also affect your feelings, moods, and actions.

"You have come through treatment," says Meg Gaines, patient advocate and director of the University of Wisconsin Center for Patient Partnerships in Madison, Wisconsin. "You have survived. Do you know why that is important to you? What do you do with your life now to make survival worth it? And how do you make sure you have a high enough joy quotient?"[22]

Amber

It's weird to be healthy. You really don't know what to do with yourself. I was sick for five years, so to be healthy again is a weird feeling. It doesn't even feel right. You have to learn how to live without limitations because for so long, I had reasons why I couldn't do things and go places. Now that I can do things, it's overwhelming.

I don't really know how to become an adult because all those years that I was supposed to be transitioning into adulthood—I felt like I was being held back by cancer. Now I feel like I'm thrust into the world, but I didn't really learn what I'm supposed to do next with my life. I had to act like an adult when I was younger, but I don't have a lot of basic skills.[23]

Amber, nursing student and leukemia survivor. *Courtesy of Amber Luchterhand.*

* * *

Cancer and its treatments can make you weak, scared, and helpless. It can steal your developing sense of independence and disrupt your relationships and your plans just at the time when you want to be defining yourself, thinking about relationships, and exploring career choices. It takes you out of the setting of school, activities, and sports where you should be testing your social skills.

Instead, you have been developing survival skills. You've been fighting for your life, and you've had to take on a lot of serious responsibility, so it may be hard to reconnect with friends who are worrying about broken nails and big dates.

Your feelings and worries can seem crushing if you try to keep them in, and it's important not to let them get toxic. There are people you can talk to. Social workers, psychologists, and clergy are trained to help you. Share your feelings with

---

☑ **POPEYE WAS RIGHT— EAT YOUR SPINACH**

Leafy green vegetables may help protect against lung cancer in current and former smokers, according to early research supported by the National Cancer Institute reported January 12, 2010.

Researchers in Albuquerque, New Mexico, studied cells that were coughed up by more than a thousand current and former smokers. They were looking for methylation damage on two genes that have been linked to lung cancer. (Methylation is when a small molecule called a methyl group is added to other molecules and may change the way those molecules act in the body.) Then the researchers analyzed what the test subjects ate. Those subjects who ate more leafy green vegetables had a reduced level of the kind of gene damage by methylation.

The next step in their investigation, according to the researchers, is to learn more about how methylation works so it can be used for early detection of lung cancer. They also want to learn more about how diet can raise or lower our risk of getting cancer.[24]

relatives and other adults you trust. Find a cancer support group in your area.

Peter

Originally, I couldn't really understand what was happening. The first six months to a year I was completely emotionally overwhelmed. Just going from moving out of the house to go to school, and then going back to living at home till I was twenty years old—and seeing everyone I graduated with moving away. I felt like I was being left behind, but I never felt like giving up.

I think I'm still getting to the point of feeling like a survivor. It's a big adjustment. I went through three years of treatment and surgery, on and off every few months. To finally hit that two-year remission was really huge. I've relaxed a little more. I feel like I can really focus on living, but it's always in the back of your mind, especially how many times it has come back for me. But this is the longest period I've had since my diagnosis.

Your support system changes over time. I have a lot of friends, and we are all figuring out what we are going to do with our lives. I live with one of my brothers. I have an older sister in town. I communicate with my parents at least every week, and I still e-mail with my doctor. Now it's different support, but I think I still rely on it.

Part of being a survivor is allowing what you've been through to make you reflect and understand what other people may be going through.[25]

*   *   *

CANCER RISKS IN THE ENVIRONMENT

Things in our environment like viruses, sunlight, and chemicals act on our cells every day of our lives, and some of them make changes in our cells that can lead to cancer. These cancer-causing agents are called carcinogens.

Whether something in the environment increases your chance of getting cancer depends on how long you are exposed to the substance and other issues such as your genetic makeup, diet, lifestyle, health, age, and gender. For example, diet, alcohol consumption, and certain medications can compromise the chemicals in your body that normally break down cancer-causing substances.

Researchers still don't really understand why you might get cancer while the person next to you who received the same exposure to a carcinogen does not. Exposure to cancer-causing substances is only part of what makes one person get cancer while another does not. Scientists believe that there may be some protective genes or other factors such as fruits and vegetables in the diet that help prevent disease.

Every two years, scientists from a wide range of government agencies and educational institutions publish a report on carcinogens that lists more than two hundred agents known or suspected to cause cancer.

The list includes the following:

tobacco

diet

alcoholic drinks

ultraviolet radiation

viruses and bacteria

ionizing radiation

pesticides

medical drugs

certain chemicals[26]

There are more details about all these carcinogens in other sidebars throughout this book. You can also find them listed in the index.

No one wants to get cancer. No one is glad that he or she is a cancer survivor, but as tough as treatment can be, you may find that the experience has made you a stronger person. You've gotten a crash course in what is important in life and how to take care of yourself. You may feel a sense of purpose that some of your friends will never find.

Juliette

Now that I'm not sick, I'm back on the track team, and I also do forensics. I actually did a speech last year called Giving a Gift. It was a speech about presenting the gift of hope to other kids who have cancer.[27]

Seth

It was a long journey, but I got through it. I'm a new person, and I love life. Before, in high school I was always worried. Am I going to say the wrong thing? Are people going to like me for who I am? But what is great about me now is that I'm not afraid to talk to people. Just be yourself. That's what I found out. Some people may not understand, but most people will.

I think some people take life for granted. People get mad about little things, but you should cherish those little things because you don't know if something like cancer is going to happen. You don't know if your life will be taken away the next day, so you have to live every day to the fullest. I don't care who you are. You have to be aware of that.[28]

* * *

NOTES

1. President's Cancer Panel, *Living Beyond Cancer: Finding a New Balance*, President's Cancer Panel 2003–2004 Annual Report, p. 5, deainfo.nci.nih.gov/advisory/pcp/annualReports/pcp03-04rpt/Survivorship.pdf (December 8, 2010).

2. Libby Falck, interview with author, September 4, 2008.

3. Amber Luchterhand, interview with author, October 4, 2008.

4. U.S. Department of Health and Human Services, National Cancer Institute, and National Institute of Environmental Sciences, *Cancer and the Environment: What You Need to Know*, NIH Publication No. 03-2039, August 2003, www.cancer.gov/images/Documents/5d17e03e-b39f-4b40-a214-e9e9099c4220/Cancer%20and%20the%20Environment.pdf (accessed March 24, 2010).

5. National Cancer Institute, "The Childhood Cancer Survivor Study: An Overview," updated August 11, 2009, www.cancer.gov/cancertopics/coping/ccss (accessed January 4, 2010).

6. President's Cancer Panel, *Living Beyond Cancer*, p. iv.

7. President's Cancer Panel, *Living Beyond Cancer*, p. 52.

8. National Cancer Institute, "The Childhood Cancer Survivor Study."

9. Paul Sondel, presentation at Kids with Courage IV, at Monona Terrace Community and Convention Center, Madison, Wisconsin, July 5, 2008.

10. National Children's Cancer Society, *The Mountain You Have Climbed: A Young Adult's Guide to Childhood Cancer Survivorship: Beyond the Cure*, p. 3, www.nationalchildrenscancersociety.org/NetCommunity/Document.Doc?id=51 (accessed March 24, 2010).

11. K. C. Oeffinger, A. C. Mertens, C. A. Sklar, et al., "Chronic Health Conditions in Adult Survivors of Childhood Cancer," *New England Journal of Medicine* 355, no. 15 (October 12, 2006): 1572–1582.

12. National Cancer Institute, "Late Radiation Therapy Side Effects," *Radiation Therapy and You: Support for People with Cancer*, posted April 20, 2007, www.cancer.gov/cancertopics/radiation-therapy-and-you/page9 (accessed March 24, 2010).

13. Peggy Possin, coordinator of the University of Wisconsin–Madison Hospitals Long-Term Survival Clinic, interview with author, August 6, 2008.

14. U.S. Department of Health and Human Services, National Cancer Institute, and National Institute of Environmental Sciences, *Cancer and the Environment*.

15. Falck, interview.

16. Possin, interview.

17. Peter Greenwood, interview with author, August 20, 2008.

18. U.S. Department of Health and Human Services, National Cancer Institute, and National Institute of Environmental Sciences, *Cancer and the Environment*.

19. Luchterhand, interview.

20. Juliette Walker, interview with author, September 7, 2008.

21. Greenwood, interview.

22. Meg Gaines, presentation at Kids with Courage IV, at Monona Terrace Community and Convention Center, Madison, Wisconsin, July 5, 2008.

23. Luchterhand, interview.

24. National Cancer Institute, "Diet May Protect against Gene Changes in Smokers," posted January 12, 2010, www.cancer.gov/newscenter/pressreleases/Dietaryfactorslungcancer (accessed March 26, 2010).

25. Greenwood, interview.

26. U.S. Department of Health and Human Services, National Cancer Institute, and National Institute of Environmental Sciences, *Cancer and the Environment.*

27. Walker, interview.

28. Seth Paulson, interview with author, August 26, 2008.

RESOURCES

The government's Medicare website has information about whether you are eligible for Medicare and how to enroll.

www.medicare.gov/MedicareEligibility

Medicaid is health insurance that helps many people who can't afford medical care pay for some of all of their medical bills. Learn more at this website.

www.cms.hhs.gov/MedicaidEligibility

This video, prepared for the Children's Hospital Los Angeles, is about the meaning of cancer for a teen.

www.youtube.com/watch?v=1BxUMDgsyG0

Survivor Alert is a website providing information that every young adult cancer survivor needs to know.

www.survivoralert.org/

Beyond the Cure's website has information for survivors of childhood cancer.

www.beyondthecure.org/

The National Coalition for Cancer Survivorship (NCCS) offers a series of Cancer Survivor Toolboxes to help you deal with the challenges of surviving cancer. Each toolbox includes an audio program you can listen to online or order as a set of free CDs. NCCS also offers booklets on topics such as talking with your doctor, health insurance, and employment rights.

www.canceradvocacy.org/resources/resources-order-form.html

At the CureSearch website you can learn about how to support yourself and others physically, mentally, and emotionally. This website lets you customize the information to your cancer type and age.

www.curesearch.org/for_patients/aftertreatment/survivorship/

CureSearch also has a resource directory of national insurance assistance.

www.curesearch.org/resources/resourceservice
.aspx?ServiceId=10

The Children's Oncology Group has long-term follow-up guidelines for survivors of childhood, adolescent, and young adult cancers that you can download.

www.childrensoncologygroup.org/disc/LE/default.htm

The Patient Advocate Foundation is a national nonprofit organization that serves as an active liaison between the patient and his or her insurer, employer, and/or creditors to resolve insurance, job retention, and/or debt crisis matters relative to his or her diagnosis through case managers, doctors, and attorneys. Patient Advocate Foundation seeks to safeguard patients through effective mediation assuring access to care, maintenance of employment, and preservation of their financial stability.

800-532-5274
www.patientadvocate.org

You need to create your own comprehensive follow-up program, and the American Childhood Cancer Organization's website can show you what this program should include.

www.candlelighters.org/Information/followupprograms.aspx

Teen Roll Call

You can learn more here about the teens and young adults who generously shared their experiences as cancer survivors.

KENZIE DERR

Kenzie was diagnosed with cancer, and her left leg was amputated above the knee when she was seven years old. "I was done with chemo by the time I was nine," she remembers, "and everything seemed like it was okay. Then when I was fourteen, my right ankle started hurting." Doctors found cancer in her other leg. Kenzie started chemo again but had to have her right foot amputated too. "I ended chemo right after I turned sixteen, and I've been in remission for a year and a half now." Kenzie has also benefitted from a bone marrow transplant of stem cells harvested from her own bone marrow.

"I've definitely learned a lot from my second cancer," she says. "Before, I was miserable and self-conscious about my one fake leg. I would pity myself. I guess before my second cancer, I thought this is the worst thing that could happen to me. The second cancer made me realize that we should be thankful for what we have now. It's given me a different outlook on life. I came up with a phrase that I put on my hospital door. People would sometimes do a double take as they walked by. It said, 'Footless but not defeeted.'"[1]

LIBBY FALCK

Diagnosed with bone cancer in her right leg when she was five, Libby went through treatment and surgery. Seven years later she was diagnosed with a different kind of bone cancer in the same place, which might have been caused by her original radiation therapy. She spent another year and a half in and out of the hospital in treatment. "I was hooked up to an IV 24/7 the whole time," Libby remembers. "Chemo is dreadful, but you have no choice. It's just what you do."

"I do have some limitations with my leg now," she says. "I can't run very well, but it works surprisingly well for all it's been through."

In college Libby created a documentary film about teens and cancer called *White Walls* and formed a support group called Teens Tackling Cancer. She graduated from college with a degree in communication arts and is currently working with AmeriCorps helping young people with physical disabilities learn to sit ski at the National Ability Center in Utah. After attending cancer camp, she became a counselor to help other young people. "I loved being a counselor," she says, "and because of camp, I have the job I have now."[2]

JON MICHAEL GABRIELSON

Now a sophomore at the University of Wisconsin–Madison, Jon Michael was diagnosed with acute lymphoblastic leukemia when he was seven. "I collapsed while crossing the street while coming home with my sister from first grade. Later that weekend, I went sledding, and I could hardly get up the sledding hill. There was an extra burden weighing me down. The next morning, I couldn't move my legs. They were really painful. Within two days, they diagnosed it."

Jon Michael's treatment lasted almost two years—much of which he spent in a hospital far from his home. "I'm 20 now. Cancer filled the first half of my life. So much happened during that time, but what stands out is the acceptance of other kids in the hospital. We all had different illnesses, but we would hang out in the lounge and watch movies together. It really shaped who I am."

As a senior in high school, Jon Michael ran for mayor of his town. "I was really shy. I didn't talk to anybody before I got cancer, then I really had to talk to a lot of adults. I learned my social skills in the hospital. As an extension, I got my leadership skills from that."[3]

ADDIE GREENWOOD

Addie spent her high school years helping her brother Peter fight for his life against recurring cancers. Because his condition was so often really risky, Addie says, "I felt like I had to be with him every possible moment. As time went on, I felt sort of afraid to move on with my life and move far away or even out of town, because he wasn't able to. This was a time when he should have been starting college. Then I got to that age, and he was still at home and in the hospital a lot. I was very hesitant to do what I was supposed to be doing at that time. It seemed very important to me to be there with him."

Now that Peter is doing well and moving on with his own life, Addie has started to build a life of her own. She saved money and has explored Eastern Europe. Her career goal is to become an oncology nurse.

"I'm glad there is more support for siblings out there now," she says. "I don't remember being offered any info while I was going through this just a few years ago. I think it could have helped a lot."[4]

PETER GREENWOOD

Peter accelerated through high school, graduated, and started college a semester early. Then his knee began to give out on the basketball court, and he was diagnosed with bone cancer. His knee was replaced with an artificial joint, and a tough regimen of chemotherapy stopped the cancer. After Peter started college again, the cancer returned in his lungs.

To fight the cancer, he went through several lung surgeries and had his leg amputated. "My oncologist said, based on how I'd responded to chemo before, I had a 30 percent chance of surviving," says Peter. "That was two years ago. I feel like I'll be dealing with this for the rest of my life." After three years of recurring cancer and five years of not being sure if he would live, Peter is starting to look forward and plan his life. He has been a volunteer counselor at First Descent, helping cancer patients learn to kayak. "Having a common experience with a bunch of other survivors is really good," he says. "[You] get that communal feeling right away working on something that is hard to do."[5] He is interested in a career in psychology so he can put his experience to use helping others who must travel their own rough roads.

BRITTANY HILL

Brittany was very sick for two years before being diagnosed with acute myelogenous leukemia at age fourteen. Finally, after a series of tests, she was rushed by ambulance to the hospital, and her life hung in the balance for twenty-four hours while her blood was removed, cleaned, and returned. "I was watching myself while they were doing all this stuff to me," she remembers. "I felt like it wasn't even me, and that was just my first night." She remained in the hospital for seven months.

This is Brittany's fourth year in remission. "I'm good on the cancer part," she says, "but I have other medical issues from the side effects of the treatment. Now I have to see every doctor in the world because of all the organs that the chemo messed up." Because she is still not very strong, Brittany postponed post–high school education for a year. "I want to be a chef. I had trouble eating in the hospital. One day my mom decided to cook for the hospital in the hospital kitchen. Seeing the joy that it brought to people to have a home-cooked meal made me want to cook for other people. I'd like to see both the hospital patients and the people who are visiting them eating well."[6]

AMBER LUCHTERHAND

Amber was diagnosed with leukemia when she was fourteen. She spent two and a half years in chemotherapy. Six months after the treatment was complete, at age seventeen, Amber relapsed. "The scariest time was when I got a blood clot," she says. "The doctors told me they were going to put me to sleep. I told Mom to tell Dad and Megan, my sister, that I loved them. I really thought that was the end of it."

Amber is in remission now, off treatment, and studying to be an oncology nurse.

I had a lot of complications with chemo. They didn't know what to do with me because my side effects were so bad. But I did want to live, so I had to fight. It was worth it. I mean all of it. It was worth it. The stories that I have now, even though they are sad sometimes, they can give people hope.

I was sick for five years, so to be healthy again is a weird feeling. You have to learn how to live without limitations again, and I have a goal. When I was sick, all my nurses were a source of encouragement. I think having a nurse who can relate to you is really important. I think I can do that.[7]

MEGAN LUCHTERHAND

Megan has learned to live with cancer in her family as she helped her older sister battle leukemia. "Generally all I knew about cancer is that you can die," Megan remembers. "That's pretty much what I thought when my parents told me about Amber because that's what I saw on TV—that people with cancer died."

Besides trying to take care of her sister, Megan had to learn how to take care of herself while her parents poured their time into keeping Amber's spirits up. "I definitely grew up fast," says Megan. "Watching someone go through cancer helps you understand that life is precious, and you can't take anything for granted."

Writing about her feelings in a memoir (an excerpt is included in this book) helped Megan deal with how cancer hit her family. "At first it was about telling the story about what had happened," she says, "and by the end, it helped me realize how I had grown, and how Amber had grown, and how we had grown as a family."[8]

AMANDA NICHOLLS

During her first year of high school, Amanda was diagnosed with cutaneous T-cell lymphoma. "I have been to so many different hospitals. All they can do is slow it down. I'll be on treatments for the rest of my life, unless they come up with a cure. I didn't spend much time in the hospital, but I've been on chemo pills and steroid creams. Right now I'm on a break from treatment."

She has continued to attend school and hold a job throughout. "I've learned to mature," Amanda says. She has learned to balance school and work, deal with money issues, and take care of her health by eating well and trying to get enough rest. "It's made me a better person," she says, "and I'm more serious now than I used to be. I'm going to try and get a scholarship so I can be a pediatric oncology nurse practitioner. I want to use my cancer as a way to teach people."[9]

PRISCA PATRICK

Prisca was diagnosed with a brain tumor when she was fifteen months old. "I've been told millions of stories about that," she says. "I was walking with a tilt, but my doctor thought it might be a stomach virus because that's what my brother had. My mom took me to one more doctor who said it was meningitis or a brain tumor. The tumor was the size of a tangerine. There was so much fluid in my brain because the tumor had blocked the way the fluid should move. Everything was damaged. I had to learn to walk and talk again."

The brain surgery has left scars on Prisca's head and neck, and she has a shunt (or tube) to keep fluid from being trapped in her brain. "When I was growing up, I couldn't do gymnastics or cheer leading. I couldn't turn upside down because of my shunt." Prisca has had repeated surgeries to maintain the shunt. She is also coping with late effects of her treatment as a college student. "I just found out about late effects, and I've been pretty frustrated, but I'm trying to pull back and get everything straight," she says. Prisca is finance major with a dream of running a day care program for children with disabilities. Her advice is "Once you do survive cancer, you want to live life— not just survive it."[10]

SETH PAULSON

As a college freshman, Seth needed his best friend to drive him to the doctor's office because he was having chest pain and trouble breathing. His doctor sent him straight to the hospital. "When they first put me in the ambulance they didn't use the sirens, but when we got deeper into Madison that's when they turned the sirens on, and that was pretty heavy," he remembers. Seth was diagnosed with B-cell large diffuse lymphoma, and learned to his relief that not all cancers are fatal.

"I kept going to school while I was going through cancer treatment. I was doing activities. I didn't let cancer affect me because I knew I was going to get through it, and I knew my cancer was a fast cancer. I didn't let it stop me." He is now cancer free and completing a degree in graphic design. "It was a long journey, but I got through it. I'm a new person, and I love life," says Seth.

"When you go through cancer, when you first learn about it, your first thought is, 'Am I going to die? What's going to happen with my future? Do I even have a future?' You have to look past that. You have to look at the sky and not at the ground. Being happy with what you've got. That's pretty much it."[11]

CHASE PROCHNOW

His mother was diagnosed with breast cancer when Chase was sixteen and with leukemia when Chase was eighteen. He had to learn how to take charge of his own life while his parents focused on his mother's recovery. "It was different in our home," Chase remembers. His mother went to the hospital and didn't come back home for a month and a half.

Chase learned everything he could about the specifics of leukemia so he could understand better what was happening to his mom. He also took more responsibility for himself. "It forced me to grow up through a tough situation," Chase says. He feels fortunate that he had a good support network from school and church to see him through. "I think it's important to cling to the things that you are close to. My football team in high school supported me. I had a close group of friends that I held tight with. I belong to a small church with close ties, and my friends and family friends and extended family really came together."[12]

CHELSEA PROCHNOW

Chelsea was eighteen and had just started college when her mother was diagnosed with breast cancer. When Chelsea was twenty, her mother was diagnosed with leukemia. She learned to balance college with the responsibilities of holding her family together. "At such a young age, I wasn't expecting to be taking care of my parents," she says. Chelsea wanted to be a bone marrow donor for her mother, but her uncle was a better match.

"I know cancer takes lives," Chelsea says. "I have lost friends and other family members to cancer, but I never doubted that my mom would come home. She had this incredible energy that was contagious. It was hard not to feel good about yourself and good about life even though you were surrounded with tragedy and terrible illness."[13]

For a time, her mother's illness put a barrier between Chelsea and her college friends because Chelsea felt they could not really understand the burden she was experiencing. In the long run, Chelsea believes those of her friends who went through the experience with her have a new and more positive perspective. Chelsea has finished college and is working with Teach for America.

JUSTIN THOMAS

A promising high school athlete, captain of both football and wrestling teams, Justin tried to play through the pain until he was diagnosed with non-Hodgkin's lymphoma right after his seventeenth birthday. When he finally went to the emergency room, Justin was diagnosed and started on treatment immediately. "Because I'm an active person—to be in bed all day is not my style. I hated being constricted. The nurse was always looking for me because I was always out of my bed," he admits. Justin's treatment included three surgeries and eight months of chemotherapy that changed his life. "I had everything going for me with sports," he remembers. "I had to change my life plan really quick. I started writing poetry and songs, and I auditioned for a play."[14]

Justin made the most of his new life by acting in school plays and serving as president of the Interact Club, which takes on community clean-up jobs, and of GUMBO (Groups Understanding Multiple Blends of Students). An A student, Justin also mentored academically challenged students through the Big Brothers/Big Sisters program. He was named one of the Alabama Public Television Young Heroes of 2008. Now a college freshman, Justin is majoring in theater in Birmingham, Alabama.

JULIETTE WALKER

Doctors found a tumor on one of Juliette's ovaries when she was sixteen. Her tumor was a rare form of cancer, and Juliette found herself going through round after round of intense chemotherapy while isolated from friends and even the comfort of her gray tabby, Cleo. "It progressed and got worse," Juliette remembers. "I wasn't ready for it all. It was really hard to see myself look that weak."

"I felt like I had to be a baby the whole time," she says. "If anything went wrong I had to call the doctor or go into the hospital. . . . I really liked having my mom there during the night, even though as a teen you feel like you should be more independent."

Juliette worked hard in summer school so she could graduate with her class. She has put her cancer behind her and is attending college in California. "Everything feels completely normal. The only thing I can tell [is different now] is I'm on the swim team and my times are not so fast but I'm part of the team, and I enjoy that."[15]

NOTES

1. Kenzie Derr, interview with author, December 21, 2009.
2. Libby Falck, interview with author, July 11, 2008.
3. Jon Michael Gabrielson, interview with author, December 7, 2009.
4. Addie Greenwood, interview with author, December 17, 2009.
5. Peter Greenwood, interview with author, August 11, 2008.
6. Brittany Hill, interview with author, December 21, 2009.
7. Amber Luchterhand, interview with author, December 4, 2009.
8. Megan Luchterhand, interview with author, December 7, 2009.
9. Amanda Nicholls, interview with author, December 13, 2009.
10. Prisca Patrick, interview with author, December 21, 2009.
11. Seth Paulson, interview with author, August 26, 2008.
12. Chase Prochnow, interview with author, December 10, 2009.
13. Chelsea Prochnow, interview with author, August 27, 2008.
14. Justin Thomas, interview with author, December 15, 2009.
15. Juliette Walker, interview with author, September 7, 2008.

Glossary

acupuncture (AK-yoo-PUNK-cher) The technique of inserting thin needles through the skin at specific points on the body to control pain and other symptoms. It is a type of complementary and alternative medicine.

aspiration (as-per-AY-shun) Removal of fluid or tissue through a needle.

benign tumor (beh-NINE TOO-mer) A growth that is not cancer. It does not invade nearby tissue or spread to other parts of the body.

biopsy (BY-op-see) The removal of cells or tissues for examination by a pathologist. The pathologist may study the tissue under a microscope or perform other tests on the cells or tissue.

bone scan A technique to create images of bones on a computer screen or on film. A small amount of radioactive material is injected into a blood vessel and travels through the bloodstream; it collects in the bones and is detected by a scanner.

cancer (KAN-ser) A term for diseases in which abnormal cells divide without control and can invade nearby tissues. Cancer cells can also spread to other parts of the body through the blood and lymph systems.

carcinogen (kar-SIN-o-jin) Any substance that causes cancer.

carcinoma (KAR-sih-NOH-muh) Cancer that begins in the skin or in tissues that line or cover internal organs.

CAT scan A series of detailed pictures of areas inside the body taken from different angles. The pictures are created by a computer linked to an x-ray machine. Also called CT scan.

cervical cancer (SER-vih-kul KAN-ser) Cancer that forms in tissues of the cervix (the organ connecting the uterus and vagina). It is usually a slow-growing cancer that may not have symptoms but can be found with regular Pap tests (a procedure in which cells are scraped from the cervix and looked at under a microscope). Cervical cancer is almost always caused by human papillomavirus infection.

clinical trial (KLIH-nih-kul TRY-ul) A type of research study that tests how well new medical approaches work in people. These studies test new methods of screening, prevention, diagnosis, or treatment of a disease. Also called clinical study.

colorectal cancer (KOH-loh-REK-tul KAN-ser) Cancer that develops in the colon (the longest part of the large intestine) and/or the rectum (the last several inches of the large intestine before the anus).

germ cell (jerm sel) A reproductive cell of the body. Germ cells are egg cells in females and sperm cells in males.

human papillomavirus (HYOO-mun PA-pih-LOH-muh-VY-rus) A type of virus that can cause abnormal tissue growth (for example, warts) and other changes to cells. Infection for a long time with certain types of human papillomavirus can cause cervical cancer. Human papillomavirus can also play a role in some other types of cancer, such as anal, vaginal, vulvar, penile, and oropharyngeal (the part of the throat at the back of the mouth, including the soft palate, the base of the tongue, and the tonsils) cancers. Also called HPV.

immunodeficiency (IH-myuu-noh-dih-FIH-shun-see) The decreased ability of the body to fight infections and other diseases.

infertility (IN-fer-TIH-lih-tee) Not being able to produce children.

intravenous infusion (IN-truh-VEE-nus in-FYOO-zhun) A method of putting fluids, including drugs, into the bloodstream by inserting a tube into a vein. Also called IV.

laparoscope (LA-puh-ruh-SKOHP) A thin, tube-like instrument with a light and a lens for viewing. It may also have a tool to remove tissue to be checked under a microscope for signs of disease.

laparoscopic surgery (LA-puh-ruh-SKAH-pik SER-juh-ree) Surgery done with the aid of a laparoscope.

late effects Side effects of cancer treatment that appear months or years after treatment has ended. Late effects include physical and mental problems and second cancers.

lethargy (LEH-thur-jee) A condition marked by drowsiness and an unusual lack of energy and mental alertness. It can be caused by many things, including illness, injury, or drugs.

leukemia (loo-KEE-mee-uh) Cancer that starts in blood-forming tissue such as the bone marrow and causes large numbers of blood cells to be produced and enter the bloodstream.

lymph (limf) The clear fluid that travels through the lymphatic system and carries cells that help fight infections and other diseases. Also called lymphatic fluid.

lymphedema (LIM-fuh-DEE-muh) A condition in which extra lymph fluid builds up in tissues and causes swelling. It may occur in an arm or leg if lymph vessels are blocked, damaged, or removed by surgery.

lymph gland (LIMF gland) Tissue that filters lymph fluid and stores lymphocytes (white blood cells).

lymphoma (lim-FOH-muh) Cancer that begins in cells of the immune system.

malignant (muh-LIG-nunt) Cancerous. Malignant tumors can invade and destroy nearby tissue and spread to other parts of the body.

melanoma (MEH-luh-NOH-muh) A form of cancer that begins in melanocytes (cells that make the pigment melanin). It may begin in a mole (skin melanoma), but can also begin in other pigmented tissues, such as in the eye or in the intestines.

methotrexate (meh-thuh-TREK-sayt) A drug used to treat some types of cancer. Methotrexate stops cells from making DNA and may kill cancer cells.

methylation (meh-thul-AY-shun) A chemical reaction in which a small molecule called a methyl group is added to other molecules. Methylation of proteins or nucleic acids may affect how they act in the body. The addition of methyl groups, which are simple four-atom molecules, to DNA can affect whether the gene is expressed, that is, whether the gene's signal to produce a protein is actually sent. Many genes involved in critical cell functions, including cell division, are methylated in lung tumors. Gene methylation is likely to be a major mechanism in lung cancer development and progression, as well as a potential marker for the early detection of lung cancer.

MRI (also called magnetic resonance imaging) A procedure in which radio waves and a powerful magnet linked to a computer are used to create detailed pictures of areas inside the body. These pictures can show the difference between normal and diseased tissue. MRI makes better images of organs and soft tissue than other scanning techniques, such as computed tomography (CT or CAT scan) or x-ray. MRI is especially useful for imaging the brain, the spine, the soft tissue of joints, and the inside of bones.

oncologist (on-KAH-loh-jist) A doctor who specializes in treating cancer.

osteosarcoma (OS-tee-oh-sar-KOH-muh) A cancer of the bone that usually affects the large bones of the arm or leg. It occurs most commonly in young people and affects more males than females.

Pap test A procedure in which cells are scraped from the cervix for examination under a microscope. It is used to detect cancer and changes that may lead to cancer. A Pap test can also show noncancerous conditions such as infection or inflammation.

pathologist (puh-thah-loh-jist) A doctor who identifies diseases by studying cells and tissues under a microscope.

port An implanted device through which blood may be withdrawn and drugs may be infused without repeated needle sticks. Also called port-a-cath.

remission (ree-MIH-shun) A decrease in or disappearance of signs and symptoms of cancer. In partial remission, some, but not all, signs and symptoms of cancer have disappeared. In complete remission, all signs and

symptoms of cancer have disappeared, although cancer
still may be in the body.

sarcoma (sar-KOH-muh) A cancer of the bone, cartilage, fat,
muscle, blood vessels, or other connective or supportive
tissue.

shunt A passage that is made to allow blood or other fluid to
move from one part of the body to another. For example,
a surgeon may implant a tube to drain cerebrospinal
fluid from the brain to the abdomen. A surgeon may also
change normal blood flow by making a passage that leads
from one blood vessel to another.

spinal tap (SPY-nul tap) A procedure in which a thin needle
called a spinal needle is put into the lower part of the
spinal column to collect cerebrospinal fluid or to give
drugs. Also called lumbar puncture.

stress The response of the body to physical, mental, or
emotional pressure. This may make a person feel frustrated,
angry, or anxious, and may cause unhealthy chemical
changes in the body. Untreated, long-term stress may lead
to many types of mental and physical health problems.

thyroid cancer (THY-royd KAN-ser) Cancer that forms
in the thyroid gland (an organ at the base of the throat
that makes hormones that help control heart rate, blood
pressure, body temperature, and weight).

tissue (TISH-oo) A group or layer of cells that work together
to perform a specific function.

tumor (TOO-mer) An abnormal mass of tissue that results
when cells divide more than they should or do not die
when they should. Tumors may be benign (not cancer) or
malignant (cancer).

ultrasound (UL-truh-SOWND) A procedure in which high-
energy sound waves are bounced off internal tissues or
organs and make echoes. The echo patterns are shown
on the screen of an ultrasound machine, forming a
picture of body tissues called a sonogram. Also called
ultrasonography.

Index

About the Author

Denise Thornton is a seasoned newspaper journalist and environmental blogger who holds a master's degree from the University of Wisconsin–Madison School of Journalism and Mass Communication with an emphasis in science writing. She focuses on translating technical topics for general audiences, especially young readers. Denise was a bone marrow donor to her brother, who died of leukemia as a young man, and is personally familiar with the ways cancer can wound teens and their families and how to cope with its challenges.